Young, Dumb, and Impatient

Megan Roberson

RIVER BIRCH PRESS
Daphne, Alabama

Young, Dumb, and Impatient
by Megan Roberson
Copyright ©2021 Megan Roberson

All rights reserved. This book is protected under the copyright laws of the United States of America. This book may not be copied or reprinted for commercial gain or profit.

Unless otherwise identified, Scripture is taken from *THE HOLY BIBLE: New International Version* ©1978 by the New York International Bible Society, used by permission of Zondervan Bible Publishers.

ISBN 978-1-951561-74-1 (print)
ISBN 978-1-951561-75-8 (ebook)

For Worldwide Distribution
Printed in the U.S.A.

River Birch Press
P.O. Box 868
Daphne, AL 36526

*To the beautiful princesses and princes in my life,
my daughter, Imani Roberson,
and my niece, Janice Brown,
and to my two sons,
KJ and Kash Roberson*

As you all grow and experience life for yourselves,
it is important to always sit back and
lean unto the understanding of your heavenly Father
and not man (Proverbs 3:5-6).

Allow His Presence and protection to flood your hearts
so the decisions that you will be faced with are pure,
sound, and consistently aligned with the plan
that Christ has set for your lives.

You four are beautiful, loved, blessed, and highly favored.
I encourage you all to be better than I ever was
and do God's best in everything you do.

I speak health, purity, wisdom, and wealth into your lives.
God has and will always have you covered.
Mommy/MeMe loves you all very much.
May God always bless you all.

Contents

1. Megan Brown! *1*
2. Teenage Trials *10*
3. College Bound *19*
4. Mommy Life *32*
5. Love and Marriage? *50*
6. Army Wife, Army Life *60*
7. Impatiently Lost *75*
8. Wheeeere's God? *89*
9. Feelin' Myself Again *97*
10. Full Circle *103*

Introduction

In today's world, everything and everyone seems to run on speed and convenience, from food, to service, to education, and careers. People have embedded certain goals and marker points in their lives so that important tasks are completed. If they aren't completed, people feel it is either the end of the world or they will find a way through hell or high water to make it happen. I know because I was one of those people. I valued myself on my accomplishments of set goals so that I would not be a statistic.

I had to learn that as children of God, true friends of Jesus Christ, we can always achieve our goals and will never be a statistic, and He will be highly exalted over all names (Philippians 2:9). Because it took me so long to really trust and not rush the process, I wasted valuable time and missed out on many experiences in my life.

One thing that some people have twisted ideas about is their time. If we trust the timing of the Holy Spirit and not man, then we will remember that it's never too late to achieve what we may feel is impossible because with God all things are possible (Matthew 19:26).

I encourage you today as you take time and read this book to reflect on things you may normally rush through, allow God to search your heart, and set your watches back to HST—Holy Spirit Time—and enjoy where God has placed you in whatever moment you are in. God bless you.

One

Megan Brown!

    I have always felt that I was meant to do something great, even as a child. I was extremely social, outgoing, and ambitious. Anything that I wanted to achieve, I did! The blooming of Megan Brown all started in the small town of Lawton, Oklahoma. My family and I lived in a cozy three-bedroom home in a very friendly neighborhood. My siblings and I made a lot of friends, and my parents were pretty well known because that's where they grew up too.
    Although I was happy, I often noticed my mother on most days wasn't too joyful. She worked and my father stayed home with my siblings and I because he was medically retired out of the military. I never witnessed them fighting much, but I often felt they were disconnected from one another.
    Since I was the oldest, I felt compelled to make my parents happy. My mom never liked a messy home, so I woke up early to make sure the house was clean, dressed, and did as much as I could to lighten the parental load. I unknowingly began to take on different responsibilities and made it my job to fix things, which later in life bit me in the behind.
    Although I was social and outgoing, I was an extremely stressed out child. In order to relax, I felt things needed to look a certain way at home. I became so used to cleaning and being independent that I forgot I was a child. The responsi-

bilities I put on myself were technically not mine. My parents saw my work and the effort I put in our home and often rewarded me, not to mention they were always happy with me when I took initiative to complete chores. I began to feel like I had to do these things for my parents to be happy with me.

As a child, I didn't know the meaning of unconditional love. I often heard that love was an action word. So, I did as much as I could to win over the affection of my parents. If I didn't complete a task, I felt they weren't going to be happy or proud of me. The funny thing is, as I began to yearn for the validation of my parents, I also began to feel a spiritual presence. Not knowing much about God, I had a strong desire to get to know who the Almighty was.

The Brown family didn't go to church much, if at all, but we were taught to pray—the usual grace at dinner time and bedtime prayers. I found myself praying to a God I really didn't know. I wanted to attend church so I could get to know Him better. I thought this would help me gain clarity on what I was feeling.

On Sunday mornings, I woke up early, got dressed, and went into my parents' room saying, "I'm ready! Are we going to church this morning?" My mom would be on the phone, and my father, in and out of sleep, would laugh and verbally escort me out of their room. As I mentioned before, I was very ambitious and got what I wanted, so I began going to church with my grandparents. On first Sundays, I saw the congregation take the Lord's Supper. I noticed that not everyone took it, which was because they had not been baptized. I knew then that I wanted to be a part of what I felt was this exclusive, cool club! I felt if I were baptized, I would understand why this strong holy Presence was in my life!

At the age of six I was baptized. I was proud that I got to take the Lord's Supper with everyone else! But unfortunately, something was still missing. I didn't feel complete. I thought God was mad at me because I wasn't doing anything for Him. In Sunday school, we were taught that God is our heavenly Father. I then made a connection between my father in heaven and my father on earth. I decided that if I did things to make my father on earth happy, then I needed to do things to make my heavenly Father happy also.

Shortly after I was baptized, my grandmother, the one I sometimes attended church with, passed away. About a year or so later, my life was back to having late Sunday brunches, playing outside, or doing anything but going to church. The yearning to get to know God slowly faded away, but I noticed that I began to have disturbing dreams and felt frightened at night. Until then I had felt a Presence of something powerful, loving, and strong, but now I felt a different presence—one that made me question who I was.

I soon began to develop fears and thoughts that a seven-year-old shouldn't like thoughts of dying. I felt sad and was overly sensitive and frustrated. I tried to communicate with my mother, but she didn't understand my feelings; my dad listened, but I didn't think he really understood either. I felt emotionally burdened and taught myself how to distract my thoughts by cleaning and doing multiple chores around our home.

At the age of eight, my family and I relocated to San Antonio. To make a long story short, I hated it, but my mother seemed to be in a better place mentally there. She was working and we lived in a nice area. She and my father were getting along, and they were happy. My siblings seemed to adjust well also.

Unfortunately, it wasn't the same for me; I just did not want to be there. I was often depressed and I wanted to go back to what I knew—a nice friendly place, with a great school, and kids I grew up with! But I had to quickly get over my feelings because I was the oldest and the responsible one—the sibling who fixed things!

My father made it known that since we lived in a bigger city, I must be an example, help around the house, and watch over my siblings. I was responsible for waking my two younger siblings up for school in the morning, for making sure the apartment was cleaned before my mom came home from work, and for getting my homework done. All that would seem to be a lot for an eight-year-old to take on, but I was determined to stay in the good graces of my parents, no matter what.

I still managed to get rewarded and continued to make them happy, but I wasn't happy. The yearning of wanting to know God came back, but the dark presence that introduced itself in Oklahoma seemed to follow me to Texas and wouldn't leave. Due to my unhappiness, I often had dreams that I was jumping off the balcony that overlooked the parking lot in our apartment. I would sit in my room and try to talk myself back into being happy. I wanted to fix myself! I needed to fix myself so my parents wouldn't think I was crazy. I was Megan Brown, the leader, the eldest of the Brown kids, the one in charge when Mom and Dad were gone, and I couldn't let this presence overtake me.

As months passed, I finally adjusted to being in Texas. I began to make friends, and I felt more like my old, outgoing self. I felt somewhat happy again. As I began to make friends and become comfortable with living in San Antonio, I noticed that the friends I made were girls with long, pretty hair who dressed very well. It was as though my insecurities were looking for any reason to come out and make themselves known.

I began to feel a bit masculine. I was a girl with her hair in corn roll braids, basic clothes, and a mustache. I didn't feel good about myself at all. It didn't make it any better that I wore glasses and had a major case of acne. Every time I looked in the mirror, I felt horrible. I mostly blamed the move to San Antonio as the reason for my awkward physical appearance. It eventually became hard for me to truly be myself. I allowed my insecurities to get the best of me, which turned me into not liking who I was.

I now know that the enemy feeds on the negative feelings we put out into the atmosphere. As a child who wasn't planted in a spiritual foundation, I didn't know how to fight back and remind myself who I was and whose I was. I didn't know how to counteract the manipulation of the enemy with the power of God. Instead, I played the games of the flesh and invited the enemy to prey on my negative feelings of insecurity, depression, doubt, fear, anxiety, frustration, and loneliness. As these feelings festered inside me, I felt the presence of what I know now as the enemy in different areas of my life as well as my family.

Since my mother worked, the responsibility of making sure my siblings and the house were clean fell on me, at least I felt that way. Not only did I have to hide my feelings, but I had to make sure everyone and everything was okay in order to keep the peace in the home. If the house wasn't clean, my mother would be upset with my father, and he would get upset with us kids. My siblings didn't listen to me, so I just got things done on my own.

As I picked up more responsibility, I developed more negative feelings of anger and resentment. I felt upset with my siblings but most of all with my parents. I was upset with my mother for not understanding me and my father for not being present. He was there physically, but sometimes he seemed to check out, leaving me to pick up the slack.

I felt I was to blame when things went wrong. Therefore, I needed to do what I could to make sure everything went right. Due to the negative emotions that began to fester inside me, I often got in trouble for having a bad attitude. My attitude was really a frustration that stemmed from the imbalance in our home. In the Brown family household, the children were taught to stay in their place. I didn't have the authority to address my parents in any kind of way. Due to the fact I was unable to speak, my feelings came out through my attitude.

Although I was young, I felt I had been blessed and cursed with a mature spirit. I was tuned in to the feelings and energy of others. I had opportunities to observe the different outcomes of situations within my family. Looking back now I thank God because I feel He was giving me teaching moments. He showed me what not to do and how He can take care of my circumstances in life when I strive to trust Him.

As the years progressed, I felt like I had the world on my shoulders. There was an undying battle that took place within my spirit and flesh. I was completely aware that my family and I needed to be grounded in the Word of God. For some reason, we had a hard time getting there as a unit. Because we were all scattered within ourselves, I was vulnerable to relationships, situations, and emotional issues that affected me all the way into my adulthood.

Even now as an adult, I still remind myself that everything that goes wrong isn't always my fault. I can't be so hard on myself. We just can't control some things that happen. As children of God, we have to give our burdens unto Him.

Give your burdens to the Lord, and He will take care of you. He will not permit the godly to slip and fall (Psalm 55:2).

Only He, God Almighty, can be the fixer of all things. We weren't created to solve every problem or find all the solutions.

Let's Do a Quick Recap!

So it may seem like I was a dramatic child…maybe. But, what we should understand is that from the minute we are birthed into this world, darkness is waiting to latch onto us and suck out the life that God has so graciously given us because we are born into sin.

Surely, I was sinful at birth, sinful from the time my mother conceived me (Psalm 51:5).

We are all made with a purpose, and the enemy knows that. I was born with a calling on my life, and because I didn't know how to get in position to put on the armor of God, I was growing up ill-equipped for battle. Ephesians 6:10-11 says that we must be strong in the Lord and in His mighty power. We must put on the full armor of God so that we can take our stand against the devil's schemes. If we aren't prepared, the enemy will come in to steal our joy and the hope the Lord has planted inside of us (John 10:10).

He doesn't care how young or old we are. The enemy began to attack me at the tender age of six through my mind, emotions, and identity. I went throughout my childhood questioning who I was, not liking myself, and mad at my family for not protecting me from some situations that occurred. I needed someone to minister to me, someone to show me how to pray and love God first, so that He may show me how to love myself and others.

We love because He first loved us (1 John 4:19).

It was important for me to share the beginning stages of my life here because that is where seeds were planted. The term "seed" is a metaphor used to refer to the words, circumstances, and people that are implanted in our lives. They can be filled with either life or death. We are put on this earth to be seed planters, to sow seeds of love into each other's gardens (lives). For those of us who have children or wish to start a family one day, no matter how young they are, the enemy doesn't care. He will take the life of an innocent child at any moment, prowling like a lion, waiting for someone to devour (1 Peter 5:8).

Although the enemy is present and waiting, he can be defeated through the love, prayers, and teachings from the adult figures in our family. The beginning stages of our lives are important because we as children tend to imitate the lifestyles around us through our behavior. For example, as a child I yearned for the understanding of God, but my parents weren't spiritually available. I was left interpreting my emotions on my own, which invited insecurities from the enemy because I was open to deceit. God designed the family to represent His Kingdom, therefore it is up to the adult figures to pour into the lives of their children in a positive way.

We must be on guard and alert, nurturing and praying for

our children daily. Our children are a heritage from the Lord, the fruit of the womb, a reward (Psalm 127:3). It's important that we encourage their gifts and plant seeds of love into their gardens! We should try to be walking, living, breathing testimonies for our children through the word of God.

Let's remember that no matter what we went through as children, or how much we felt no one seemed to care or listen, God is bigger than all of that. He was with us the entire time; that's why we are still here. We're given another day, filled with grace, to open our hearts up to Him and surrender our lives so that we can experience Him for ourselves.

The Lord your God is in your midst, a mighty one who will save; He will rejoice over you with gladness; He will quiet you by his love (Zephaniah 3:17).

Two

Teenage Trials

Now that we have covered the lonely years of my childhood, let's speed up into the lovely life of an off-balanced, hormonal teenager. (Sighs, while sarcastically thinking, "Oh joy.") At sixteen, I had a driver's license, felt kind of cute, and was getting noticed by boys! I would like to admit that I was undercover boy crazy, just a little. I described myself as having a boyfriend before I even knew what having a boyfriend meant. It was tragic.

When I was sixteen I began dating a boy who is now my handsome husband, Kionicio (pronounced Kuh-Nee-See-Yo). He and I met in middle school and reconnected as friends during our freshman and sophomore year of high school. We started dating our junior year, which was the start of a premature blessing that would eventually change my life forever.

I spent a lot of time with Kionicio, and we began to connect on a level that was a bit unhealthy for teenagers. I held onto a lot of insecurities and tried to be someone I wasn't with other people; but with Kionicio, it was different. He encouraged me to be myself as we talked about God and even started going to church together. We became so close that the topic of sex came up—every parent's nightmare.

The habit of fixing things became so apparent in my life

that I became a pro at fixing myself. As I think back, the term "fixer" for me was nothing more than a fraud. I was just someone with the ability to put on a mask or cover things up. I buried my hurt, depression, anxiety, guilt, and shame deep inside. No one, not even my boyfriend who knew me for four years, could tell what I had been hiding. Because of my ability to hide my shame, he thought I was a virgin and respected me for that.

Due to how I carried myself, a lot of people saw me as a conservative, sweet young lady and assumed I was a virgin. Unfortunately, I wasn't. A couple of years before Kionicio, I found myself experiencing some heavy peer pressure. In my freshman year of high school, I enjoyed a new social setting that was both fun and free. I wanted to feel included and accepted by my peers.

Sexual activity seemed normal, and it was as though if you weren't sexually active, you weren't normal. I didn't have a true understanding of my relationship with God. I wasn't aware of how special our temples are and that sex was made to unite a man and woman for the dual purpose of the procreation of mankind and to serve one another in a safe, secure, and intimate way. When we're impatient and rush into things prematurely, not only are we risking the chance of parenthood, but we're creating a recipe for unnecessary pain and guilt.

From what I experienced, I thought I would learn from my past mistake, right? Wrong! Kionicio and I became sexually active months into dating. No one knew; we didn't flaunt it. We hid it or should I say we both became fixers by protecting our reputations. We wanted to cover up our season of fornication so people wouldn't think negatively of us.

As I stated in the previous chapter, I didn't like myself in my younger years and not much changed in my teenage years. I masked my insecurities and negative feelings with makeup, clothes, and outings with my friends. I distracted myself very well, and I played right into the enemy's plan.

When we find ourselves yearning to live for God and called into relationship with Him, our biggest tests and trials will occur. At this time since my relationship with God was on autopilot, the Holy Spirit inside of me became dormant, allowing my flesh to drive me in my decision making. Instead of addressing the issues I had, I hid them, ignoring what was holding me back from a true deliverance.

During my time of hiding, my parents finally came together and decided to put God first. We joined a church as a family, and things began to rapidly change in my life. Although I was still carrying the heavy weight of my flesh, that feeling of gentleness that I felt as a child began to overflow in my body again.

Every time we went to church as a family, I became less and less heavy, silently releasing the dead weight that followed me from my childhood into my teenage years. When I sat in the services, I saw people in the choir and in the congregation who seemed so bright and free! I wanted to look and feel like that. The yearning to experience the power of God rekindled. I was in the process of full submission, ready and willing to serve God with all my heart.

Now notice that I said in the *process* of full submission. It should be easy for me, right? Of course not! At the time I was sixteen, almost seventeen years old, still trying to fit in. I made the process harder than what it had to be because I was still trying to fix myself. I wanted to hide my transgressions instead of laying them at the cross. With being so young and having this burning desire to know the love of God, I needed to talk to a seasoned worshipper—someone who could tell me the truth in love and guide me to a voluntary place of repentance at the altar.

I was too ashamed to come out of my cave of darkness. I allowed the enemy to torment me into seclusion. It's so important for us to listen to the Holy Spirit when He tells us not to be afraid.

> *Come to me, all who are weary and burdened, and I will give you rest. Take my yoke upon you and learn from me, for I am gentle and humble in heart, and you will find rest for your souls. For my yoke is easy and my burden is light* (Matt. 11:28-30).

This verse is so beautiful because it's God giving us permission to come as we are and know that nothing is too big or problematic for Him. He doesn't want us carrying around heavy loads of guilt, shame, insecurity, loneliness, depression, sadness, and any other sinful emotions or habits that we as fleshly beings like to hide.

I pray right now that God puts people in our path who are seasoned worshippers, lovers of Christ and His Word. I pray He sends us people who can encourage us to a voluntary repentance as well as confess what has been holding us back from a spiritual breakthrough. Remember a confession isn't all about getting right with God but an opportunity to release, reflect on the goodness of God, and invite Him into our hearts for a makeover that will change our lives!

Now back to me finding the path of submission. Church services were phenomenal. My family and I learned so much!

We began to grow as one, and even my siblings and I were becoming closer. We were bonding over what we learned. We even shared how we were going to be accountable for one another. The more we went to church, the more time we found ourselves serving in ministry.

I was a part of the youth choir and took part in Bible study and Sunday school. My spirit began to thirst more and more for Christ. I found myself getting excited as well as becoming knowledgeable of the Word. For the first time in my life, I felt like I belonged. Ministry, serving, praying, worshipping, listening, smiling, and fellowship seemed so natural to me like I was born to be a part of the body of Christ.

I guess the growth in me didn't go unnoticed because I soon found myself obtaining the privileges of directing and leading songs in the youth choir, occasionally teaching Sunday school and Bible study classes, as well as building wonderful relationships with the beautiful girls I mentored. I seemed to be finding myself and really understanding who Christ was in my life until that is, church was over.

It seemed like as soon as I left church, this feeling of loneliness and being misunderstood would consume me again. Imagine being a teenager and being the odd one out. Because I gave God permission, He was having His way with me. I was changing. To me it seemed good, but to those around me, it was weird.

While the growth process in me was taking place, my relationship with my boyfriend was becoming strained. I wanted to talk about church and have Bible study while he was more interested in basketball, as well as dealing with some other issues I wasn't aware of at the time. I began to lose friends and associates because our interests were different. Although I made relationships at my church, I still felt alone.

In the eyes of most, I appeared to have it all together. I was this sweet young lady who just loved the Lord! People didn't realize there was an internal battle brewing inside of me. I know now that once again the enemy wanted me badly. He wanted to trick me into thinking people didn't want to be bothered with me because of the love I had for God. He tricked me into thinking I was doing too much, singing too much, speaking too much, encouraging too much, praying too much, and shining for God too much.

All the insecurities I had let go were slowly returning. Instead of being excited about serving God, I started to feel fear. I was so scared that I would have high anxiety from the day before I had to teach, speak, sing, or direct the choir. Of course, it seemed like a normal case of the nervous jitters. When our mind is creating thoughts of failure and reminding us of our past, we begin to feel we're not good enough. Then our focus is directed away from our tasks to what people might say or think and any other negative thoughts that come our way. The enemy is just trying to distract us out of our opportunity to serve and minister to others. Our nerves should never overpower the completion of the tasks God gives us.

Unfortunately, once again I fell into the enemy's trap to dim the light God had put inside of me. I turned to what every other teenager turned to, a distraction, which was for me, a job. I worked at the movie theater and silently hoped that the job would occupy my Sundays so I wouldn't have to commit to a leadership role at church. I fell right back into the shallowness of my flesh that drew me away from church, which was my connection to spiritual growth.

As I began to become more familiar with my job, I liked it. I had fun. I made myself available to work every chance I got. I had my boyfriend, Kionicio, a car, my own little money, and I soon changed my priority list so that God was not at the top. The more I drew away from God, the more I became comfortable with the idea of acting out in the flesh. Galatians 5:17 says,

> *For the flesh desires what is contrary to the Spirit, and the Spirit what is contrary to the flesh. They are in conflict with each other, so that you are not to do whatever you want."*

If we know who Jesus is and accept Him as our personal Savior, it is apparent that our new life has been established under grace to allow Christ to grow us up spiritually through His Word, prayer, and fellowship. As a result, our spirit will become strong, and we will learn how to denounce the flesh and not be so quick to fall into temptation, giving in to what it wants. Of course, no one wants to intentionally entice their flesh and do the opposite of what God requires. Unfortunately, it becomes a habit and eventually a way of life when one is carrying emotional baggage.

We all have insecurities that manifest in different things and affects us in different ways. For example, some people may not know how to express themselves, so they bottle up every insecurity and bury them. They allow the enemy to convince them that they are strong and don't need to talk to anyone because they may seem weak to others. That's never a good idea. It is one of the biggest tricks the enemy can ever play on us! If we were never seen as weak, then how can Christ work through us and make us strong? (2 Cor. 12:9)

Feelings that we tend to harbor will eventually turn into pride, depression, anxiety, anger, and anything else that is the opposite of the glory of God. Harboring these feelings will leave our hearts surrounded by a spiritual barbed wire fence, making it extremely difficult to receive or give the love of Christ.

Recap Time!

Throughout this chapter there has always been a constant battle within my flesh and spirit, a battle that will never die as long as we live. As we go through life, God gives us opportunities to become stronger and denounce our flesh by reading as well as acting on His Word.

Being a teenager is challenging because the mental, physical, and spiritual parts of the body are developing the foundation of adulthood. The enemy is calling dibs on our interests and wants to taint the gifts and abilities Christ has ordained inside of us. Remember that when there is good, evil is always present (Romans 7:21). I'm not going to lie and say following Christ and denying the flesh is 100% easy, but I do know it is well worth it!

I pray that God takes us in whatever spiritual or physical state we are in and turns us completely around! I pray that God gives us the strength to tap into our God-given abilities and take hold of the new life Christ has for us. For in Him we will find all things new, life more abundantly, and a fresh beginning.

I pray we receive our kingdom blessings and be in a position to bless others the way Christ would. He wants to bless us in every way, spiritually, physically, financially, professionally, and personally. Once again, I speak life over us, decreeing and declaring that bondage, chains, and generational curses on us will be broken, stopping the enemy in his tracks, leaving him powerless over us and our families!

> *And pray in the Spirit on all occasions with all kinds of prayers and requests. With this in mind, be alert and always keep on praying for all the Lord's people* (Ephesians 6:18).

Three

College Bound

When I completed my senior year of high school, I realized that I was going to be entering a whole new world—I was going to college! Unfortunately, it wasn't the school of my choice, but I was optimistic that everything would be all right. I was still battling spiritually and to stir up even more things inside of me, all the seniors at my church were asked to speak during church service.

It took me two weeks to meditate over God's Word and receive direction on what He wanted me to speak about. I closed myself off, and as I blocked out the distractions I was holding onto, I began to remember why I had fallen in love with Jesus. He began to unveil His plans for my life, giving me insight on how I could prevent these situations in the future. He encouraged me to pray, stop trying to figure things out on my own, and trust Him.

The very first Bible verse that I stored in my heart and continue to follow to this day is Proverbs 3:5-6.

Lean not to your own understanding but in all your ways acknowledge Him and He shall direct your paths.

Now that I was preparing to leave the nest, God was teaching me that I must stay away from the philosophy of man (Colossians 2:8) and allow the Holy Spirit to interpret things for me. As we begin to trust God by following His path for our lives, we will find that God will help us by giving us wisdom. This wisdom will result in peace of mind and most importantly, the discernment to make sound decisions.

During my time of meditation and reconnecting with the Lord, He kept telling me to pray about going away to school. While I prayed, I remember having an uneasy feeling, like God was encouraging me to be still and wait instead of rushing away to school. I talked with my mother about my thoughts on possibly finishing my basic courses at home, but she was convinced that I was supposed to go to a four-year school right after graduation.

Once again, I got distracted, this time by the opportunities of campus living, forming new relationships and bonds with my peers, as well as unsupervised freedom! Graduation came and went, the summer flew by, and before I knew it, I was driving to San Angelo, Texas, with my father and my personal belongings in the backseat of my car.

I attended San Angelo University, a small school compared to others, not a lot going on—no Greek life, not many activities—and I was extremely disappointed. I found myself falling into a silent depression. I was often anxious, and I never really felt like I belonged at that school. As I allowed disappointment to fester in my spirit, I found myself covering my negative feelings with my puppy love for Kionicio! While I was in San Angelo, he was in Lubbock, which was three hours away. I had a car, and almost every weekend I was at his campus or he was at mine. We were in love, acting grown up, and yet being dangerously irresponsible.

After three months of being in college and traveling back and forth to Lubbock, naturally my convictions began to

College Bound

catch up with me. I started experiencing a spiritual starvation. At the time, I wasn't listening to worship music, going to church, or having any type of quiet time with the Lord. I had caused my spirit to become weak due to the fleshly desires I had indulged in. I was lying to my parents every weekend, fornicating, and simply making decisions to do the opposite of what my spirit yearned for—surrendering to the love of Christ. I found myself unhappy and wanting to go home.

I was trying to fit in, but because the Lord dwelled in my heart, it didn't work. The lifestyle I tried to take on seemed good for a minute, but I found myself constantly seeking for something new because I was dissatisfied. We should remember the one who can fill the void in our lives is Jesus. He doesn't want to cause us eternal boredom but to impact our lives so that we may be dynamic for His Kingdom!

Before I formed you in the womb I knew you, before you were born I set you apart; I appointed you as a prophet to the nations (Jeremiah 1:5).

Since I was called into a relationship with God at an early age, it wasn't easy for me to ignore His presence for long. I knew I needed to spend time with my heavenly Father. At the time I had another young, strong woman of God in my life, who was my best friend. She was my accountability partner.

We prayed together, confided in one another, and encouraged each other. As she and I grew in the Lord, others began to join us in our journey. Next thing I knew, we had a group of people going to church with us! As things were changing around me, God allowed me to meet another young woman who became my roommate. Since she and I lived together, we too became close, and I saw that spiritually we were in the same boat—struggling with our flesh to get to something greater!

By now the holidays were approaching, midterms were ending, and I remember feeling extremely uneasy. I went back home and I felt a dark cloud in the air, a heaviness that followed me around during the entire holiday break. Of course, I thought it was my nerves and I ignored it, distracting my feelings with the love and warmth of my family.

I went back to church and felt light! I was home, right where I wanted to be, where I needed to be! Our holiday break soon came to an end, and there was a delay in my going back to school. While my friends were back in San Angelo, I was home, anxiously waiting to leave. After a week or two, I went back to school, only to feel that heaviness even worse! I didn't feel right, and I knew things were in the process of changing.

As I settled back into my dorm, I was disturbed. I couldn't rest or find peace. I happened to look in my student account to register for my courses and all I saw were these huge red letters, saying that I had a balance that needed to be paid ASAP! My heart dropped, of course I did what every young adult with no responsibilities does—call on Mom! I called and told her what was going on, and in a calm voice she said she would handle it.

When we got off the phone, I began to put it all together, thinking to myself, "Oooh okay, so that's why I got delayed from going back to school—my tuition wasn't getting paid!" Since I developed a close spiritual bond with my roommate, I told her everything. She encouraged me through prayer, and we found ourselves along with my best friend fasting to receive direction from God. We took time to rejoice in the Lord as well as talk to one another about the importance of God in our lives. I couldn't afford any distractions! I needed to be in God's presence so I could receive His direction.

While we were fasting, I got a call from Kionicio—how convenient. I told him about the fast my friends and I were attempting to complete, but he wasn't too enthused or seemed to care that much. Later that night he called only to break up with me. I laugh about it now because it got dramatic. I didn't understand why he called to break up with me!

While I was fasting, doing the good work of the Lord, he was finding himself and exploring life outside of our relationship. Our breakup was done for a purpose. I had asked God to remove all distractions, and at the time my biggest distraction was Kionicio. I found myself wanting to please him more than God.

Our focus shouldn't be on pleasing man but directed to God so He can love us into becoming stronger people to do His will. I had to respect Kionicio and where he was coming from because he respected me. He knew how important my relationship was with God, and he didn't want me to choose. He was honest with himself in knowing that a relationship with God wasn't a priority for him at that time.

No matter who we share a relationship with, when God is the foundation, He will help us see things more clearly. We will have the wisdom to make decisions based on His direction through His Word rather than ourselves. Our goal as believers is to be Christ-centered and not self-centered. If we are constantly operating in self, we are not giving God enough room to work through us so that others may see His light and not our own.

Christ is a gentleman, always giving us the free will to make choices. His Word says,

I love those who love me and those who diligently seek me will find me (Prov. 8:17).

For those who are not ready to seek God, don't force them, judge them, or make them feel bad. We should continue to pray for them while seeking God for ourselves, and He will then show up and use us in a mighty way for the sake of others.

After a horrible night of crying my eyes out with my best friend, we decided to shake it all off and prepare for our spring courses. We went to the library to pick out courses and register, or so I thought. I logged into my student services account only to find out that my account was still past due! Just the thought of it still makes me cringe. I immediately felt my stomach in my toes, and my face flushed with a huge red heat that spread all over the inside of my body.

I told myself to breathe, get it together, that there must be some sort of mistake. I looked over to my friend and said, "Girl, I'm going to run to the restroom really fast, I'll be right back," with the fakest smirk and shakiest voice ever heard. I rushed off to the restroom and called my mom. The conversation was short and sweet, "Oh don't worry about it, I'll take care of it." After living with my parents for 18 years while being an observing child and later knowing that God has gifted me with a discerning spirit, I could easily tell when something wasn't right. My phone call ended, and I began to feel sick. I knew then that I had to find peace within myself and prepare to go back home.

After three days of waiting in my apartment for the ques-

College Bound

tion of "to leave or not to leave" to be answered, God just told me to leave. I remember calling my parents, telling them not to worry and that I'd just come home. When my mother, not ever wanting to give up, said, "No, just give me some time, you don't have to leave," I knew it was time.

I packed up my room, loaded my car, said my goodbyes to my sister friends, and drove three hours back home in silence. I felt lost, defeated, confused, overwhelmed, angry, but most of all, embarrassed. I was the oldest of three. I was supposed to be the example, the leader, the first one to go to college and make something of myself. I couldn't help but think, what am I going to do at home?

I reached home and when I walked in, I was greeted by my father telling me to get my attitude together because I didn't need to make my mom feel bad. Hearing him say that really got me upset, but it triggered my instinct to fix it. Thoughts began to rush in my head, *I have to get back in school, I have to pay my debt, I have to get a job, I have to move out, I have to help my parents, I have to be a leader for my siblings, I can't be a bum, I, I, I, I!* I felt so many emotions and fears.

I immediately forgot who I gave permission to lead me—God. I just got dumped by the guy I cared a lot about, I had to leave school, and now I can't even be mad? It didn't seem like God was handling things too well, so maybe I just needed to help God out a little. I mean God was busy, He had a lot of people's problems on His plate, so I thought, *Don't worry God, sit back and chill, I got this one. I mean I can clean up my own life, right?*

Wrong! Please know that we can't fix anything as I told you in the previous chapters. When things begin to pile up on you, it is the best time to sit and be still. Was God responsible for the bad things that were happening? Of course not! But what He can be responsible for is turning it all around for His good.

> *And we know that in all things God works for the good of those who love him, who have been called according to his purpose* (Rom. 8:28).

The most important reason why we must sit, be still, and hear His voice is so that He can navigate us through the hard times. If He isn't navigating us, we will lean on our own understanding, opening the doors to the deception of the enemy when it comes to our decision making.

Because I was leaning on my own understanding, I was carrying around depression, anxiety, guilt, anger, resentment, and frustration. I would see my college friends on social media having fun, being young and free, and I was home, taking my siblings back and forth to school. Instead of allowing God to use me and seeing things from a different perspective, I was stuck in a self-made funk!

Tired of being at home and feeling hopeless, I started applying for jobs. I had to find a way to pay off my debt so that I could go back to school. I put my application in at many places, but none of them was calling back fast enough. I decided that I was going to see a recruiter for the military. My parents kept telling me to be patient and pray to God, but I didn't want to hear that. The funny thing is on the same day I was supposed to visit the recruiter, I got a phone call from one of the jobs I applied to. I felt like I could breathe again.

Things were finally looking up. I was reminded then that God's hands were controlling my life because I asked Him to be the head a long time ago. When God makes promises over our lives, He doesn't break them. Things may look challenging, but if we can be still and know that He is God (Psalm 46:10), our outcome will be victorious!

Being grateful that God took care of me as He promised, I spent a lot of time with Him. During my time with God, He began to show me the importance of trust, structure, and obedience. I made a list of my bills and the goals for my life. After I wrote everything out, I began to pray over it and slowly but surely God allowed me to pay off what I needed to pay in a matter of months. We are reflections of Christ in every area, even our finances. God wants to supply our needs and make sure that we understand the importance of being disciplined and paying what we owe.

Let no debt remain outstanding, except the continuing debt to love one another, for whoever loves others has fulfilled the law (Rom. 13:8).

God wants us to be free in Him in every way so that He can fill us up with His love that we may pour into the lives of others. If we're constantly stressed with our own issues, it can be hard to encourage others and be a blessing to someone else.

At the age of nineteen, I released my worries and cares to God regarding my finances, and He has made those burdens light ever since. There hasn't been anything I couldn't handle financially. God has made a way out of no way and constantly supplied my needs. I understood the importance of tithing and exercising my faith past my understanding when it came to sowing seeds for the Kingdom.

I was confident knowing that God will always do just

what He says. As I redirected my focus to God, I felt a breakthrough in my life. I realized the more I learned to trust in Him, the more I saw how He always took care of me.

I was finally in a better place, spiritually, physically, and financially. I was making goals, looking at new colleges for the fall, and feeling like a young adult should. Remember earlier in the book when I mentioned Romans 7:21

So I find this law at work: Although I want to do good, evil is right there with me?"

I found myself unintentionally playing with temptation. As I strived to stay focused on my relationship with God, I received news that Kionicio was home for summer break. We hadn't talked in a couple of months, but now that I was distraction free and focusing on Christ, he showed up. But was I disciplined enough to tell Kionicio, "Hey brotha back off, I'm livin' a blessed life, like the Clark Sisters"? Nope. I took his calls, texts, and offers for dinners. I was just pitiful.

Just as I was striving for change, Kionicio was also. He seemed different. He wasn't the sweet, quiet Kionicio I remembered from high school. His word choices were different, he took interests in outings and social groups that I was uncomfortable around, and he had become a lady's man at this point. Of course, I saw the changes in him, and I knew that God wanted me to stay focused. He didn't do all this work in me for me to regress.

I have always had a spiritual connection with Kionicio. I knew when he was going through things, I knew when something was wrong and when he needed a friend. I always prayed for Kionicio, not because I wanted him to be this saved person for me but because God allowed me to intercede for this young man at an early age. God had a plan and spoke over the lives of two individuals that He was going to bring together for the His glory, not our own.

I knew during the time of my transition and Kionicio's time of finding himself as a man, he just needed a friend. I was directed to encourage him, speak life over his situations, and most of all pray for him. Now these instructions seem simple. You can pray, encourage, and speak life into others over the phone, using social media, as well as in your individual alone time, right? Well, let's just say I began to misunderstand the instruction of the Lord.

God wanted me to be an empty vessel for Him, not an empty vessel to be used for the satisfaction of man. I began to visit Kionicio more often; visits led to hugs, hugs led to holding hands, holding hands led to pecks on the cheek, pecks on the cheek led to kissing on the lips, and kissing on the lips led to…you can fill in the blank. He and I once again fell into temptation because we were both vulnerable to the weaknesses of one another rather than our strengths.

My strength was to encourage him from afar, not up close and personal. I knew better. God is just like our parents: when they tell us not to do something, it's not because they hate us; it's because they know things we don't. They see us potentially going down a slippery slope that can hinder the greatness that is called over our lives.

That one night of reminiscing along with what started out as innocent physical interaction led to the developing of our family. At the tender age of nineteen, I became pregnant with our first baby girl.

Recap Time!

This entire chapter shows how I missed the moments to connect with Christ and hear His voice. First Corinthians 10:13 says,

> *The temptations in your life are no different from what others experience. And God is faithful. He will not allow the temptation to be more than you can stand. When you are tempted, he will show you a way out so that you can endure.*

I was tempted in my relationship with Kionicio. I also encountered temptation with alcohol, parties, and my finances. But God gave me a way out.

He always saw me through, even when I didn't have the strength or the patience to fully trust Him. He knew that I wasn't following His direction when it came to me leaving for college. He knew that going away for school wasn't going to be good for me because I didn't set myself up for success the way He told me to. Instead of holding my decision making against me, He allowed me to come home, become stronger, get a great job that increased my finances, and pay my debt so that I could prepare myself for the next chapter of my life.

God gave me a way out! He gave me an opportunity for a do-over, but once again I altered His instruction when it came to Kionicio. When God is working to make us over, He doesn't just work in one area of our lives but in all areas. He wants to search us from top to bottom so that we can become complete and mature in Him, never lacking anything (James 1:4).

I wish I was mature and patient enough to understand that back then. Instead of remembering that God has always had His hands on my life and promised me a man of God with a powerful testimony (who would one day be Kionicio), I stepped in and interrupted not only my time of grooming with God but Kionicio's revelation period. My involvement with Kionicio and the birth of our first child was not a mistake in any way, only premature.

Four

Mommy Life

By the time I became a new mom at the fresh age of twenty, I realized that what I wanted to experience in life might not happen. I felt like I was pregnant for an eternity. It was a long, drawn out, and embarrassing process. I felt like I would never reach the light at the end of the tunnel.

Sometime in the late summer, I went off to Kionicio's home. Not only did I go see him, but I lied to my family about where I was going. That is the first red flag in this story. Please remember that if we ever feel the need to lie about what we are doing, we should not be doing it. Whenever we are stuck in a tough situation and faced to make decisions, we should ask God for the wisdom we lack. He will give it to us without finding fault (James 1:5). Most of the time we ask God to show us the right thing to do, and He gives us the answers we don't want to hear. Remember that He always has our best interests at heart even when we don't understand or see what is going on.

Once my time with Kionicio was over, I immediately rushed home. The drive back to my house was extremely long and lonely. I knew I messed up. I knew something wasn't going to be right. I immediately began to pray and ask God for forgiveness. When I got home, I didn't speak to anyone. I just went to my room, covered in shame and guilt. The next morning, I had to wake up early for church. I went to the early service and tried to hide.

I thought maybe if I just attended the service and ran out, no one would notice the heavy burden of shame I was carrying. You know the saying, "What is done in the dark will come to light"? Well, what I had done the night before in the dark came to the light and busted my head wide open! My youth pastor came and sat in the pew in front of my family and asked me why I wasn't wearing my clothes to sing in the choir. The youth choir always sang at the 10:50 service, but because I felt I did something awful and wasn't worthy enough to glorify God, I didn't want to sing!

I tried to make up an excuse, but my pastor wasn't hearing it and insisted that I go home to change. I wanted to cry on the spot and just tell him "No, Pastor, I can't sing today because I'm a fornicator and a liar! I'm not worthy! I'm in need of a spiritual cleansing! I need some anointing oil!" I felt so low because I knew that the decision I made went totally against God's direction, and there were going to be some serious consequences as a result of my actions.

I had no choice but to go home and change my clothes. In between praying and crying, I finally made it back to church. It wasn't bad enough that my youth pastor made me sing in the choir but the song selection was "Wash All My Sins Away." The song is a powerful one that exposed all my sins, or so I felt. The first line of the verse says, "Forgive me, Lord, for I have sinned, I'm sorry, I'm sorry, I'm sorry."

I literally felt like a bright spotlight was on me, and there was a sign on my forehead that exposed me to everyone. The words of the song couldn't even come out of my mouth! The spirit of conviction hit me with a one, two, punch right in the gut. I felt like the wind was knocked out of me, and I just began to cry.

I remember looking at my youth pastor as he directed the song, and he stared back at me with a puzzled look of confusion. I'm sure he was wondering, "Is this girl okay?" I couldn't sing the song, I just couldn't seem to pull myself together. I felt like the song wouldn't end. I was ready to run out of the church and hide in my house. As soon as the song was over, I left.

That night I was broken! Here God was, changing my situation around. I had a good job, making money, debt free from my semester of college, and on my way to another school. I had been preparing to go to the University of Houston. I recently scheduled a visit, and I was in a good place. Only God allowed me to make it to that point. So, when I went against His direction and made the decision to not only lie to my family about Kionicio but connect myself physically with him, I knew that my slip up this time was going to be different. Something strong in my spirit was telling me to get ready.

The act that I took part in left me so heavy that I confessed to my parents about three days later. I could no longer hold this sinful secret inside. I felt sick and physically weak. I had to release what I had been holding onto. I didn't want to disrespect them any longer by holding onto this lie. It was hard for me to tell them that I slept with Kionicio because he wasn't on good terms with my family.

Although Kionicio and I dated in high school and he became part of the family, he wandered away from who he was called to be, and therefore he lost touch with my parents. While Kionicio was on his own journey, he distanced himself

Mommy Life

from them. When I released my secret to my parents, my mother was upset and disappointed. She knew my potential and what I was working towards, but most of all she didn't want me to miss out on the opportunities she did and mirror her challenges as a young woman.

My mom got pregnant with me when she was eighteen and barely out of high school. Naturally a parent wants their children to do better than they did, and having an illegitimate child, in her words, was never a part of the plan when it came to her children. I appreciated my parents for making it clear that they wanted the best for our family. They always spoke us into greatness and expected us to rise to our full potential. I knew what my parents expected out of me, which is why I was more disappointed in myself than they could ever be.

As my parents and I talked, I cried so much that I felt broken. I knew my mom wanted to get mad and curse me out, but as my mother, she had a connection with me. She has the gift not only to nurture but a special gift that allowed her to be in tune with me during that time. I believe all nurturing mothers have this gift when it comes to their children. When our mothers look at us, they seem to always tell when something is wrong.

I remember the way my mom looked into my eyes, and she knew that I was in a state of darkness. She could tell I couldn't take them being upset with me because everything they wanted to feel as parents, I was already feeling. I can honestly say if my parents didn't show me the love of God at that moment, I may not be here today.

My father asked me if I had protected myself, and I thought about it and another panic came into my heart. I said, "No sir." Just as my mother felt my pain during that moment, my dad had always had a discerning spirit when it came to his children. He confirmed what my spirit was silently preparing me for. He said, "You're pregnant."

My mom's eyes got wide and she said, "We don't know that, don't say that; it's okay, no you're not."

My dad shook his head interrupting her with his hand and said, "No, no Michelle, I know, she is going to be pregnant."

It was like God was preparing all of us in that moment. He was mentally and spiritually equipping them as my parents to protect me, guide me, and encourage me for what was to come. We ended the night with a lot of praying, hugging, tears, and most of all love.

A couple of weeks went by, and I avoided talking to Kionicio for the rest of the summer. I just wanted God to know that I was done; I changed my ways! No more slip ups! I was convinced that everything was back to normal. I even found myself getting back to that happy place I once was coming into.

I was socializing more with my peers and preparing myself for my do-over of college in Houston! To celebrate my new life, my best friend and I took a girls' trip to Austin and attended a football game. We saw so many of our old friends who went to San Angelo with us. It felt like old times. Seeing everyone was so exciting, and I couldn't help but think how much fun I was going to have in Houston!

As thoughts of excitement rushed through my brain, a rush of heat followed and took over my body. I felt faint, hot, and dizzy. I thought to myself, *I'm in the hot sun with all of my friends so maybe I'm just hungry? Maybe I just need some water? Sure, yeah that's exactly what it is, I just need to sit down and drink or eat something*. I told my best friend I wasn't feeling too good, and we ended up leaving.

On the drive home from Austin to San Antonio, I remember having a nervous feeling. I was full of anxiety. My best friend, who was part of the transition to Christ in San Angelo, knew most of my downfalls, but she didn't know how I had backslid over the summer. With her being a virgin, I didn't want to tell her what happened between me and Kionicio. The whole way home we talked, laughed, and had a wonderful time bonding. I didn't want the ride home to end. For some reason, I knew that was going to be my last time of freedom with her.

Once I got home, I felt extremely tired. My dad saw me and said, "You look drained, are you okay?"

I said, "No sir, I'm not feeling too well."

He and my mother looked at each other while trying to hold back a nervous smile. My mom jumped up and asked, "Do you want to go get a pregnancy test?"

My stomach dropped although I'd been trying to avoid what my spirit was preparing me for, I knew what the results were going to be. I didn't answer. My parents and I got in the car, drove to the grocery store, and grabbed two pregnancy tests. We returned home and before I took one of the tests, my dad held my hand, looked at me in the face, and said, "Whatever the results are, your mom and I got you. Don't worry about what people may say, you are covered with love and we will support you."

Immediately I wanted to cry and melt away in his arms. I heard everything he was saying, but the enemy was already lurking around waiting to prey on the insecurities I had been harboring my entire life.

I took one test and gave it straight to my father so he could read the results. It seemed like it didn't even take the full three minutes! The results came in so fast. My dad let out the weirdest chuckle of shock and said, "Ummm, she's pregnant!"

With the most southern accent, my mom quickly said, "You lyin'!"

My dad replied, "No, Michelle, I'm as serious as a heart attack; your daughter is pregnant."

They both looked at me, and I just stared back at them, not having the ability to truly connect with reality or digest what they were seeing and saying. My mom jumped up and said, "Here Megan, take another one."

I went into the restroom and took another one. The results of the second test seemed to come through just as fast! This time my mom held it and saw the results. She just stood there, holding back a smile of shock, nervousness, and most of all disappointment. As she looked up at me, her eyes glazed over. I could see the disappointment and hurt in them. She confirmed the test results by saying, "Well, yeah, my daughter is pregnant."

When I realized that both of my parents had confirmed what would change my life forever, I felt like I got punched in the gut all over again. I felt hurt, guilt, shame, disappointment, embarrassment, loss, loneliness, failure, insecurity, fear, and a strong unworthiness all at once. I couldn't breathe and began to hyperventilate.

I thought I saw the light, but it was the light of our ceiling fan as I was falling back to hit the floor. My parents went into prayer and reassured me that it was going to be okay.

My siblings came down from upstairs, and we ended up having a family meeting. I could barely speak. The words that did come out of my mouth were "I'm sorry." I couldn't express enough how disappointed I was because I felt like I had let my entire family down. I was the fixer. I was the oldest. I should have set a better example, but I failed.

In my mind, there was no coming back from what I did. As I thought of my immediate family, I couldn't help but think of my church family. I had another position of responsibility that I had to answer to. The Brown family closed out in prayer, and they made it clear that we were together in this no matter what. That night I could hardly sleep. I literally cried myself to sleep. I felt so low.

About two days later, my family and I had a meeting with the pastor and his wife. We talked to them and were open, honest, and transparent. The pastor suggested that I go before the church and let them know what was going on. He wanted me to understand that I wasn't a bad person, but the consequence that resulted from my action didn't align with God's Word.

I knew I needed to take some time and sit in the congregation rather than serve in the youth ministry. Some people may not agree with the decision of coming before the church and confessing or being relieved from serving, unfortunately I am not one of those people. I agreed wholeheartedly with my pastor's direction because he was only following God's instructions for my life. He and his wife both ministered to me, but most importantly corrected me in love. They didn't throw a bucket of shame on me but held me accountable for my actions, and I will always appreciate them for setting Kingdom standards and being Christ-driven vessels.

I was close to quite a few families in my church. There were so many women who played a major role in my growth and spiritual connection with God. So out of respect for them, I went to them personally, aside from the church announcement, and we had our own prayer time that prepared me for facing the church.

I will never forget the heaviness and fear I carried when I had to face the people in the congregation. I was a mentor to some of the parents' daughters; other parents entrusted me with their children. I had opportunities to speak, teach, sing, and direct the choir. Now I was being exposed as not only a fornicator but a 19-year-old girl who got pregnant out of wedlock.

The time came for me to face the church with my confession. My Brown family stood up with me, and I remember shaking. I was so nervous that when I opened my mouth, I could barely speak. Then the most amazing thing happened. The families who I was close to began to stand up from their seats and walk towards me; not only was my Brown family standing with me but also my youth pastor, his wife, my pastor and his wife, the families who I connected with, and the women of the church who made an impact in my life.

Before I knew it, there was an entire team of God's people backing me up not condoning what I did but standing up to the devil with me by casting out the shame the enemy was trying to throw at me. As they stood behind me, the Holy Spirit began to give me the right words to say. Not only did I have the strength to come clean, but through the love and support from my family, I had the strength to encourage the young people of what not to do.

When I finished talking to the entire church, we all

found ourselves glorifying God, encouraging one another, praying over one another, and releasing suppressed secrets that some people had held in for decades. God challenged every one of us to remove our masks so that He could truly search our hearts and take out what didn't align with His will for our lives.

I will never forget that moment because it reminds me every day how truly powerful God's people are when we stand together. For those of us who are quick to judge others by casting stones, remember that it's okay to hold people accountable for their actions but always allow the Holy Spirit to lead us when called to address the issues. In this way God can have the opportunity to make the corrections needed for permanent changes to take place.

The night I left the church, I was overwhelmed by the amount of love, support, and encouragement God's people showed me. I was reminded that our God is a God of love. No matter what we do, nothing can separate us from His love (Romans 8:38). God wants nothing but His best for our lives. I finally went to sleep feeling content, a feeling that I hadn't felt in a long time.

As weeks passed, I had to put things into perspective. My Brown family knew I was pregnant, my church family knew I was pregnant, and I went to the doctor who confirmed that I was pregnant. Then it really hit me, "You are pregnant! You are not going to Houston for college, you cannot hang out with your friends, and most importantly you cannot serve in ministry." Everything I couldn't do poured into my spirit. That holy high that I felt from church died down as reality began to catch up with me. I fell into a deep depression.

I was so sick that I ended up quitting my job. Every

morning, every afternoon, every night, I threw up! I couldn't hold down food, I could barely get out of bed. I was fighting not only the symptoms of pregnancy but a supernatural battle with demonic strongholds. I often had night terrors. My thoughts took me to a place of darkness. I wanted to die. I thought that my life would be better if I killed myself. Even though I felt alone, God never ceased to remind me that I wasn't.

Every night that I had a night terror, an evil thought, or felt a demonic presence, I received a phone call, a text message, or a visit from someone I was close to, reminding me that God had a plan for my life. They encouraged me to stay strong in the Lord and stand on His Word. God's power is real, the Word says,

Touch not my anointed one and do my prophets no harm"
(1 Chron. 16:22) and (Psalm 105:15).

Those of us who have been called according to His purpose will be glorified by God no matter what. When we get down and don't know what to pray for or what to do, the Lord allows His Spirit to intercede on our behalf so that all things may work together for our good because we love Him (Romans 8:26-29). Although I was in a dark place and my spirit was too weak to pray, God allowed His people to intercede on my behalf.

I felt like a complete failure. Three to four months into my pregnancy, I began to get tired of myself. I got tired of getting beat up by my own insecurities. I had to accept what reality was, take accountability for what I had done, and focus my energy on preparing to be a mother. Something precious was growing inside of me. I didn't want to make it about me anymore but about my child. I began to read the Word, pray, and make goals for myself. I wasn't working so I decided, with the encouragement of my parents, to go back to school. I enrolled at a community college and attended school full time. I began to feel my life coming back together little by little.

As I focused on changing my mindset, I still didn't want to talk to Kionicio. He knew I was pregnant, but I wanted him to focus on his education while attending Texas Tech. He wasn't in a good head space, so we didn't talk during the first trimester of my pregnancy. If anything, the absence of Kionicio during that time was a motivator for me to focus on rekindling my relationship with God. I needed Him. I yearned for the peace He had promised me and His guidance on becoming a mother.

I was determined to not become a statistic with drama, but a young woman who got pregnant, took responsibility, and provided for her child. My mindset was to live for God as He taught me how to be a spiritual, educated, and financially stable example for my baby. I began to grow because I had help during this process from a great support system at home and at church.! I was finally back on track, or so I thought.

Going into my second semester of school, I was finally able to keep my food down, I was making good grades in my classes, as well as completing hours of student teaching. Most importantly I was making it a priority to spend time with God. It seemed too good to be true. Every time I pushed forward and focused, who always popped up but the famous Kionicio.

One day I received a call from him saying that he decided to come home from Texas Tech so that he could be around for our baby. Due to the lack of conversation between us, we really didn't see eye to eye during this time. I knew that I had matured in some way because I didn't give Kionicio a second thought. I wanted to make my God proud. I knew I was living for another life, so instead of relying on my emotions, I wanted to remain steadfast in the Holy Spirit.

I told Kionicio that I didn't need help; but most of all, I encouraged him to stay in school. Although we weren't together, I loved him and cared about his well-being. Whether we were together or not, I knew God had a calling on His life, and I wanted nothing more for him but to rise to his full potential because Kionicio was and still is destined for great things in Jesus' name.

Kionicio insisted that he was coming home, and he did. While he was home, I didn't really see too much of him at the beginning; and the couple of times I did, we argued. I soon realized that seeing him was a reminder that I had messed up. I couldn't digest the fact that no matter what, I was still connected to this guy. I felt like I was a failure, and I began to become disgusted with myself all over again.

I needed my alone time. I often dismissed myself from Kionicio and appreciated his absence. That became my opportunity to regain my strength through prayer and seclusion. During this time, I often felt a sense of calmness as the Holy Spirit would reassure me that everything was going to be okay. God would speak into my spirit and tell me to cover my situation with prayer because He was working in the midst,

God is in the midst of her; she shall not be moved: God shall help her (Psalm 46:5).

I found myself being quiet and not talking a lot about a

Mommy Life

future with Kionicio. I just wanted to be a good mother. I knew what I wanted, but I wasn't sure if Kionicio knew what he wanted or even knew how to get to a place of clarity. God began to flourish inside of me; He confirmed that everything was going to be all right.

My family and I prayed all the time. We prayed about everything, day and night. My entire pregnancy was covered in prayer. Prayer changes things!

Therefore, I tell you, whatever you ask in prayer, believe that you received it, and it will be yours (Mark 11:24).

Prayer is not only about our wants and needs but the opportunity to exercise our faith and trust in God. Know that He has already fixed our problems and given us better days with bigger and better blessings ahead!

As I was becoming stronger and my pregnancy was healthy, my family and I found ourselves shifting our prayers to Kionicio and his direction. My parents gave him tough love and planted parental seeds into his heart such as instruction, advice, or encouraging words that they had given to their children. Kionicio eventually found his way back to the Brown family as well as receiving clarity from God.

He wanted to make sure he could provide for the child we created but was unsure what he should do. He spent some time talking with my parents about his future and gradually took their advice regarding joining the military. Two weeks after our daughter was born, Kionicio shipped out and was in the possession of Uncle Sam.

After Kionicio left, I went back to school and work. My dad, who was retired from the military, watched my baby, and my siblings helped too. I was extremely grateful to them but being the insecure individual that I was, I felt bad that I had burdened my family by adding a newborn baby under their roof. My guilt turned into, "I can do it by myself."

I didn't want my parents feeding, changing, holding, watching, or anything that had to do with taking care of my baby if I could help it. I often stayed in my room with my little baby. When I was home, I was an overbearing mother because my biggest fear was for my family to think I was irresponsible. I already felt they were judging me or secretly disappointed in me. I took on a giant chip and wore it proudly on my shoulder. I was a new mom with something to prove.

Due to the fact I was being so self-centered by trying to prove my imaginary point to everyone, I stole some precious moments from my parents with their first-born grandchild. I missed out on time to enjoy school and the opportunity to learn who I was not only as a mother but a young woman. I was in the perfect position to take on the support and loving advice from my parents as well as the other strong women in my life, but my pride wouldn't allow me to do so.

My spirit was extremely weak due to the strain I put on myself. I often thought, *I am twenty with a beautiful baby, no husband, a college student who lives with her parents and can barely afford all of the necessities a baby needs.* I felt so stagnant. Once again, I lost focus of God, became impatient, and wanted to fix my situation.

Weeks after Kionicio got settled in Basic Training, he sent a lot of letters. We wrote back and forth like clockwork. From the looks of his letters, I wasn't the only one wanting to fix things. Kionicio made it very clear that he wanted to provide for not only our daughter but for me as well. He wanted to get married ASAP! Of course, that sounded great. But I didn't receive it as great news. I had a mixture of thoughts and feelings.

I wanted to finish school and obtain a degree before I got married. I replied to Kionicio's letters regarding marriage by explaining my view on education and having a career. He was supportive but insisted that I could still do everything I wanted to do as Mrs. Roberson. It sounded sweet, but most of all, what about where we both were spiritually? I wasn't confident that the timing of us getting married was right. I knew I needed to pray.

I prayed but it was one of those impatient prayers, "Lord please tell me what to do, give me a sign!" It was a prayer that asked God to give me an answer right away. Sometimes God gives us answers right away, but it may not be what we want to hear so we pretend He didn't answer us. That's what I did. God showed me it wasn't time.

For example, on Sundays after church, I would call Kionicio to see if he went to church, and he would still be asleep due to a late night with his battle buddies. Another example is when the subject of growing in Christ would come up, he would get offended and say he wasn't ready for all that or that I was judging him.

I often heard crickets on the other end of the phone because he never had anything to say. I saw all the signs. God answered my prayers, but I didn't want to hear them because I still wasn't satisfied with the outcome of my decisions. I wanted to fix my life.

When we are entertaining the idea of marriage, it is important that we make sure God is leading us to the right person at the right time. Man and woman were ordained to come together to glorify the love of God through their devotion to one another. You can't come together and do anything for God if you and your significant other aren't on the same page.

After those signs were revealed, I still found myself waiting for God to tell me what I wanted to hear. Instead of waiting on God, I looked at my situation in the physical. I saw my faults. I felt that I added an extra mouth to feed in my parents' house. I blew my opportunity to attend a university. I didn't want to be an unwed mother. I wasn't growing spiritually. I felt I was losing my identity and forgot who I was striving to become. I thought maybe if I got married, these insecurities would go away. So, I decided now was the time to get married.

Recap Time!

As a young girl still trying to find herself, battling the issues of life on top of being pregnant is never easy. When becoming a parent, especially a young parent, our life is no longer our own. We really need a support system. Asking for help and being open about our feelings don't make us weak.

We can miss out on some great wisdom because we are too afraid to be transparent about what is really going on inside of us. A lot of people throw their lives away due to the issues that are weighing them down. I pray that we allow God to direct us to the right people to confide in as we humble ourselves and accept help when needed.

It is also important that we don't ever rush the hand of God, no matter what our situation looks like in the natural. Let's learn to see our situation the way God would. He is constantly molding us, so eventually our rough edges will be smoothed out to benefit His works.

If we aren't seeing things the way God does, we will miss out on an opportunity for Him to smooth something out in our lives.

Yearn for Him to lead you in His truth and teach you, for He is the God of our salvation and for Him we shall wait all day! (Psalm 25:5)

No matter how long it takes, we should be patient enough to wait because God is just that good. God loves us so much that He takes His time with us. He wants us to accomplish every goal and desire that aligns with His will. He wants us to be whole so we are not battling with any insecurities that may hinder us in life.

For those of us who may be struggling with important decisions, I pray that we allow God to smooth out the rough issues in our lives.

May God himself, the God who makes everything holy and whole, make you holy and whole, put you together - spirit, soul, and body—and keep you fit for the coming of our Master, Jesus Christ (1 Thess. 5:23)

Five

Love and Marriage?

I made the decision to take Kionicio up on his request for marriage in early September. I say it so casually because it felt casual. It didn't hit me that I was going to be his wife until I took off on a plane clear across the country to unite our new little family, but we will get to that later.

I woke up one morning, tired of the stagnation in my life and the disappointment I felt. I knew that if I married Kionicio I could right my wrong and clean up this unpleasing and shameful life I'd taken on. By this time Kionicio was at training in Arizona, approaching graduation, and preparing to go to his first duty station. We talked on the phone quite often, and every time he asked if I were ready to marry him.

After months of being persistent, I finally caved in and said, "Yes! Let's get married, everything will be okay, right?"

He replied, "Yeah, girl, you know I love you."

Now a man telling a woman he loves her sounds great. A man wanting to marry the woman he loves and take on the responsibilities a man is supposed to do is wonderful. But if we desire a Kingdom marriage, we should know that a marriage requires more than a man saying, "I love you" and a woman casually accepting because it sounds nice.

Ephesians 5:25 says,

Love and Marriage?

Husbands love your wives as Christ loved the church and gave Himself up for her.

If a husband truly loves his wife the way Christ loves the church, he must first have a relationship with Christ. When people have their own personal relationship with Christ, they have taken on the act of submission, love, transparency, honesty, and intimacy with the Lord. Therefore, when they become involved with another, there will be an understanding of humility and wholeness brought to the relationship.

I wasn't ignorant to the standards of a Kingdom relationship. I knew what I wanted in my marriage. I knew what God expected of both my husband and me. After I had already committed to marrying Kionicio, I badgered him with twenty-one questions all the way to our wedding date. (Just a side note, asking continuous questions about the same thing that you have an answer to is a sign of uncertainty. If we are uncertain about a decision or situation in our lives, we should take a step back and wait on the Lord.)

Wait for the Lord, be strong and let your heart take courage, Yes Wait for the Lord (Psalm 27:14).

Unfortunately I was far from waiting on the Lord. I had been taken over again by that "fix it" spirit. Although my family forgave me, I couldn't forgive myself. Not only was I carrying the shame of being an unwed mother, but it was a reminder of my secrets from high school, my insecurities, anxiety, worrying, and my loneliness. Being a young mother wasn't fun. I lost who I was and where I was going because I consumed myself with my beautiful baby and finding ways to mask what I was feeling.

I even managed to drown out the sound of God's voice

and direction. I would ask Kionicio to have Bible study with me over the phone; and if we did, I would tell God, "See God, all we have to do is keep You in the center and have Bible study. It's going to be okay!" The entire three months before our wedding, we probably had Bible study maybe five times.

During that time Kionicio probably attended church on his own about three times. We were separated—he was in Arizona and I was in Texas. I felt the need to remind Kionicio every chance I could that if we were going to get married, he needed to develop a stronger relationship with God on his own. He knew what I expected, and I expected him to deliver.

Kionicio and I weren't even officially married yet, and the red flags were extremely present. Let's remind ourselves that God doesn't need our help. We don't have to have the "See God, I told you so" mindset.

God is the all-knowing, even before there is a word on our tongues, He knows it all (Psalm 139:4).

God knew that I was unsure. He knew that Kionicio wasn't thinking about developing a spiritual relationship with Him at that moment. God knew that Kionicio and I both needed some grooming and maturing of our own before coming together. When God speaks, it's for us to "be still and know that He is God!" (Psalm 46:10) He is all knowing because He is our Creator and the only One who can make things right in our lives.

I began to realize that conversations regarding the Lord between Kionicio and I would often turn sour. After a while I just gave up. I mean, after all, at least I was getting married and moving out of my parents' house, right?

Love and Marriage?

My parents, on the other hand, weren't too thrilled, especially my mother. The disappointment my mother had when she found out I was pregnant turned into fear when she found out I wanted to get married. My father saw good qualities in Kionicio, but like every father, he wanted to make sure that Kionicio was going to be the considerate, loving husband that his daughter deserved.

My parents and I had a few conversations in the beginning and they all ended with "I don't know, I don't think you both are ready." Although my parents supported me during my pregnancy as well as after the birth of my child, I couldn't help but begin to feel that they were against me. I didn't want to hear what my parents had to say because I felt they saw me as a weakling, someone who couldn't take on life or responsibility. I often thought, *They already think I'm a failure so now they think I won't make it in my marriage! Huh, is that it?* I was determined to get married and once again prove this imaginary point while carrying this imaginary chip on my shoulder.

One morning I woke up feeling on fire like an adult. I asked my parents if we could talk. I said, "Mom, Dad, I understand everything you both were telling me about Kionicio and getting married, but I'm ready to marry him. I love him and we have been together since high school, and I'm ready to be his wife. You don't have to agree, but I'm willing to do this with or without your support." I said that in the most respectful tone of voice as possible, and obviously it worked because I didn't get knocked out, cursed out, or kicked out of their house.

When I was done, my parents looked at each other with a slight smile of shock and my mom said, "Well, looks like we are planning a wedding." I was silently shocked. I wondered, *What happened, why a sudden change of heart?* My dad made it clear that when I left, there would be no coming back. He said, "You want to be grown and make grown decisions. I'm going to treat you like you're grown. Don't be calling me crying to come back home because I'm going to remind you of this conversation and tell you to go work it out with your husband!" Now that's a daddy for you!

I understood and appreciated my parents for once again supporting me and loving me through my decision making. I couldn't help but be relieved that they accepted my decision. The wedding planning process went surprisingly smooth, with it being such short notice. I got so much support, encouragement, and help from my church, family, and friends. Although the process was moving and things were rolling, I was numb on the inside. I didn't really know how to feel. Were my convictions of not listening and trusting the Lord rising up? I really wasn't sure, but I knew I just needed to make it down the aisle.

About two weeks before my wedding date, my mom came into my room and asked me how I was feeling. By the softness in her tone, I knew she was being used by the Holy Spirit because my mom often speaks in truth and love with a roughness but not this time. She came in, sat on the floor, and looked at me. She began to talk about her experiences of being a young wife and mother.

She saw me mirror her and my father's actions. They both had me at a young age, my father joined the military, and shortly after, they were married. During their early years of marriage, like any other marriage, they endured some hard times, but it all resulted from them not being on the same

Love and Marriage?

page spiritually. While going through their storm, they relied on self rather than the Word of God. My mom explained that because she made decisions based on prideful emotions, she lost her identity. She missed out on opportunities and blessings from God that affected her marriage and our family.

She said, "Megan, you don't have to get married because you're disappointed in yourself. You're not a failure; your father and I are proud of the mother and young woman you are becoming." She urged me to pray and ask God for direction. She wanted me to finish school, grow more in Christ, and learn who I was as an individual.

We both got emotional, but I couldn't allow myself to tell her she was right. I was getting married because I felt like a complete failure. I was so used to masking my feelings and fixing things that I felt the need to follow through on this big step of marriage. I thought, *Yeah, my mom said she and my dad are proud of me, but how could they really be proud of their 20-year-old daughter who has a baby and is living with them?* I couldn't see how they could be proud of me. I responded by sugar coating my feelings while talking to my mom and assured her I was going to be okay.

At the end of our conversation, I looked at her and she seemed to wear a heaviness. She was scared for me. She didn't want me to delay God's greatness in my life because I was moving so fast. As a mother, I understand now where my mom was coming from. It can be heartbreaking to see your loved ones, especially your children, take an unnecessary detour in life when God has given them a clear path.

My wedding day finally came on December 20, 2009. Unlike most brides, I wasn't very excited; instead, I felt extremely numb. I didn't know how to feel. My family and I, along with Kionicio and his family attended church, closed out in prayer, then went our separate ways to prepare for what was to take place that evening. My bridesmaids and I went to go get our hair done and that turned into an all-day affair, which resulted in me being over an hour late for my own wedding.

The entire night went by so fast that it is still a blur for me. I vividly remember walking down the aisle and seeing Kionicio, who was the most handsome I had ever seen him. He got emotional, which never happens, and once we said I do, I felt light. I felt like I could finally breathe. That night Kionicio and I talked about what was next, what we expected of each other, and fantasized about how great our lives will be.

I couldn't help but thank God for His grace and mercy. His power and favor got me down the aisle. That night as I laid in Kionicio's arms as his wife, free of guilt and shame on an intimate level, I couldn't help but ask myself, "Did I marry Kionicio right now because I was crazy in love with him? I mean I do love him, a lot. We have a baby together, we have been together for a while, and we are best friends. So why do I feel weird?"

As I mentioned in the previous chapters, God wants all of us. He wants to clean out every corner and crack that may be hiding the smallest amount of residue. Yes, I was married, no longer had a child out of wedlock, and no longer had to live at home with my parents. But what about the depression, anxiety, insecurity, fear, and doubt that resided in me?

And most of all, I got married prematurely. I wondered, *Since I went against the direction of my heavenly Father and rushed His process, does that mean I won't receive the blessings He had for me, and will I reap a season of hardships that naturally comes when being disobedient?*

Recap Time!

During this chapter, it is important to see how I allowed my insecurities to turn into pride. My heart became hardened due to my own iniquities. I opened the door up to the enemy, which clouded my judgment and drowned out the voice of the Holy Spirit. Hebrews 3:13-15 talks about being deceived by sin. Verse 15 specifically states,

We should not harden our hearts as Israel did when they rebelled.

Sin brings deceit, which causes rebellion. It can be challenging to do what God encourages us to do when we are caught up in our sin because the enemy convinces us that our way is better. Our way is not better; it's longer and we will endure a lot of unnecessary bumps in the road, just as the Israelites did when they were stuck in the wilderness for forty years. Yes, in life there will be some uncontrollable hard times, but God will be right there, teaching and preparing us how to get out of it. Let's embrace our teaching moments and not take ten plus years to reach the Promised Land.

A lot of people think sin is this nasty action only categorized by killing, stealing, homosexuality, adultery, or alcoholism. That's where we can be deceived. Sin is anything that comes against the Word of God and His requirements for our lives. Galatians 5:22-23 talks about the fruits of the spirit,

But the fruit of the Spirit is love, joy, peace, forbearance, kindness, goodness, faithfulness, gentleness and self-control. Against such things there is no law.

God wants us to be at peace in every area of our lives. That "fix it" spirit that I often talk about isn't of God. It was brought on by a sinful nature that influenced me to go against God's direction. I became too impatient to wait on the Lord.

When we confess our sins, it is an act of repentance, meaning that we are open, willing, and ready to let go of what has been in the way of our relationship with God. I confessed my actions but never released my guilt and shame, which led me down a dark path of loneliness. When people who loved and cared about me reached out to help and encourage me, I couldn't receive it. The goodness of people was drowned out by the repetitive darkness that played in my head.

However, in reality I never had to prove anything to anyone. I didn't have to feel like a failure because my situation had already been forgiven and covered with the blood of Jesus and sealed with love from His people. The enemy doesn't want us to know that when God says, "I love you, I forgive you," He really means it. If we could truly trust God's Word we would begin to live freely in Christ, which allows His glory to dwell inside of us.

I feel God moving on our behalf right now. Let's let go of the guilt and shame we have been hiding. I pray God will uncover every single insecurity that we have buried deep inside our hearts and present them to the Lord. God wants to remind us that we aren't alone. If we feel that no one understands us, we should know that God understands us. I pray that God uses His people to encourage us to enjoy that place of still waters and green pastures where Christ dwells. He is waiting on us to receive His peace so that the decisions we are faced with won't be difficult for us to make. I pray we trust Him and the sooner we lean to His understanding and not our own, we will see it doesn't have to take forty years to gain our victory, for the victory is already won!

I speak blessings over our lives right now in Jesus' name.

But thanks be to God, who always leads us in triumph in Christ, and manifests through us the sweet aroma of the knowledge of Him in every place! (2 Corinthians 2:14)

Six

Army Wife, Army Life

I had now left my Brown family to join the Roberson's. I officially had a family of my own. I felt accomplished because I thought I fixed all my mistakes and the image of how I thought people perceived me. My wedding day had passed and my handsome husband graduated from training in Arizona.

We had already been married for two months when he called me up and told me that our first duty station was in South Korea. He gave me a list of things to do so our daughter and I could be with him as soon as possible. I was excited! Not only was I married, but I finally got to move out of my parents' house and raise my daughter on my own. Now I really fixed things!

Two months after completing my to-do list, I got my orders to move to Korea with my man. I was elated! The movers came and packed all my belongings, and three days later I was leaving the country. Before I left, I sat in my empty room and looked around. A thought or two rushed through my head as I hoped I was making the right decision and wishing things were going to work out with me and Kionicio.

Notice that I said wishing not praying. There is a difference between wishing and praying. Wishing is asking for something that we don't have but we desire to gain. Wishes can become begging, "Oh please let this work, Lord, please let me get this, oh Lawd I need this!" It is also a sign of uncertainty.

As lovers of the Lord and warriors for Christ, we don't ever have to beg for anything in life. Remember Mark 11:24, "Pray as if you have already received it." Also remember that "Whatever you ask in prayer, you will receive, if you have faith" (Matt. 21:22). For our prayers to manifest into something great, it doesn't depend just on God but also on our faith and trust in Him. We should believe that He has and will come through on our behalf, no matter what. I didn't leave my parents' household speaking life into my situation. I was unsure, nervous, and most of all fearful.

After a 17-hour plane ride, my baby girl and I finally reached Seoul Korea. It was amazing! We were greeted by my husband at the gate, and I was surprised by the amount of Korean words he already had picked up in such a short time. He was saying phrases to the cab driver, telling him where to go while I was allowing the culture shock to settle in. We arrived at our new home and it was the beginning of the Roberson family! We lived in an apartment in the city, and we had an amazing view. Little did I know that view was going to be used for a lot of thinking and alone time with Jesus.

Of course, when we get married we go through a season called the honeymoon period. Kionicio and I had our honeymoon period during the first couple months. We were so excited to be on our own together. During that time, we catered to one another and spent a lot of time together. It was important that Kionicio and I settle in to become one. Although

Imani was his daughter, she didn't know him due to him being away for training. She didn't let him rock her to sleep or want to be alone with him. I could tell that my baby girl was still trying to figure out what exactly was going on.

To break in our new family, we all spent a lot of time together with family meals, movie nights, and outings. Kionicio came home as much as he could during his breaks from work. It seemed like we were committed to one another. We even made it a priority to talk about our finances and other family goals. Although we were young, surprisingly we both understood the concept of what's yours is mine and what's mine is yours. One thing I can say about Kionicio is that he has never been selfish, and he was and still is a wonderful provider. From day one, his goal was to provide for our family financially; and in that area, I had learned to be secure early on in our marriage. Don't get me wrong, we had to work to get on the same page of budgeting, being frugal, and humble, but I'm grateful to say that our season of trials and understanding in the finance department was short lived. We had other fish to fry.

As I continued to settle into my new life away from home, I remembered my family saying how much fun the military life was and how I would make great friends for life and develop a support system. I was extremely optimistic and ready to mingle with other wives, make friends, and be productive in any way I could.

About a month or two after we settled in our home and received our clothes and household goods, we were off to church on the military base. I was excited! I just knew I was going to get there, meet people, and join the choir. I was thinking, "See God, I got this!" In my mind, I thought, *The first thing about being a godly wife is getting my family in church, yeeeeeaaaaas, praise Jesus!* God is good all the time, and all the time, God is good!

Now while I was puffing myself up, reminding God that I had the blueprint of what a godly family was as well as telling God what I'm going to do, I didn't realize that I was putting all my energy and focus into man. Did I love God and truly want a relationship with Him? Yes! Did I want my husband to be saved and lead our family? Yes! But for these things to happen it was for me to "draw near to God so that He can draw near to me" (James 4:8).

Remember that I took the covering I had from my family off while I was still developing as an adult in Christ. I jumped ahead of God while not listening to His direction and made my own shortcut to where I thought He wanted me to be. Soon after, God began to show me that life on my own without His covering was bad news.

Now back to my experience with church. We started attending church on base. Military style worship and service was completely new to me. In one chapel, they accommodated different religions and styles of worship at different times. For example, we attended the Gospel service. The Gospel service didn't start until 12:30 in the afternoon! I was used to church being in the morning. You start off your morning with some good word, get out of church by noon, and go on about your day. I had the wrong mindset. I looked for familiarity rather than looking for God to do a new thing (Isaiah 43:19).

This one example goes to show us that when our focus isn't on God, we allow little doses of negativity to manifest, which can potentially turn into something bigger. We then miss out on the teaching moments God has for us. I came to church with a checklist and made it all about me. I needed to uphold this image that I wanted my family to portray. Don't get me wrong, my heart was in the right place but my understanding and relationship with the Holy Spirit were still separate at this stage of my life. I still had a lot of growing to do.

Attending church service on Sundays were okay, but I still felt empty. In most churches, pastors say, "For you to be a part of the church family, you have to be involved. Join some ministries. Come to Bible study," and that's what I did. I went to Bible study and joined the choir. Immediately I felt out of place. The choir members were not welcoming, the Bible study group wasn't as warm and open as I was used to, and I felt invisible.

I tried not to let that stop me, but of course I felt a bit discouraged and was wondering what was wrong with me. On top of that Kionicio started working a lot, leaving me home alone with our baby. When he had free time, I would ask if he could attend the mid-week service with me, but he made it very clear that he was not going to go.

Although I didn't want to go alone, I tried to push through my feelings and connect with others. Making friends and mingling with people wasn't as easy as I thought. Everyone laughed and joked with one another and literally dismissed me like I wasn't even there. Instead of pressing through and keeping my focus on God, I began to dig a spiritual cave. I started to sink into a dark hole of seclusion where I could hide from rejection and the lonely feeling that always seemed to find its way back into my life. Instead of the church being my refuge, I began to seek comfort in my home, where no one could find me.

Since I was a stay at home wife and mother, I began to use my household duties as an excuse why I couldn't attend church. I soon drowned myself in my role of being a wife and mother. My job was to maintain the home while Kionicio took care of everything else. For the most part, I enjoyed taking care of our family; and to make matters better, I soon became pregnant with our second child. Four months into being in Korea, we started extending our family. I was excited, but I couldn't help but feel like something was still missing.

Pregnancy is great but can be challenging. The mood swings, emotions, appetite, and weight changes can all be overwhelming. With my daughter, I was sick a lot; but with my son, I was sad. As I progressed in my pregnancy, the honeymoon stage in our marriage faded away. Kionicio and I began to argue. He even started going out, leaving me at home, pregnant, lonely, and vulnerable with our daughter. His priorities seemed to get mixed up. He had always been a lover of basketball, so he would get off work, head straight to the gym, and play basketball for hours. Due to his busy work schedule and gym time in the evening, there would be days where I wouldn't even see him. My unhappiness quickly settled in.

Kionicio made friends and went out, while I was handling our family on my own. I had yet to make any friends or a strong enough connection with anyone who could encourage me out of the dark cave I was digging for myself. I had a lot of sleepless nights. The thought of me not wanting to be married rushed in my head. I became so bitter and full of malice that I wanted to find any reason to leave. I was so ready to go back home.

I tried to take my focus off what was going on in my marriage for a little while and get involved with the other Army wives. Well, let's just say that was a bust! I realized early on that I wasn't made to be the poster child for Army wives. These women were pros! They knew everything about their husbands' jobs, who their men worked with, upcoming training, units, ranks, and even who the First Sergeant was. I mean the list just goes on and on. Don't even get me started with all the acronyms they threw at me.

Oh, my goodness! I remember feeling extremely out of place, not to mention that some of the women's husbands were higher ranked than mine. I barely even knew my husband's rank. It was like a sorority for Army wives. I was embarrassed and out of place. I often found myself sitting in the presence of these women with my eyes squinted, just staring at their mouths, trying to understand what they were talking about. It was an entirely different world for me—a world that I didn't feel a part of.

Instead of accepting that I just didn't know these things because the army life was new to me, I took my frustration out on Kionicio. I often picked arguments with him. I asked, "Why do you always feel the need to leave me out; you don't tell me anything about work! I don't even know what your rank is or how to read it on your uniform! When were you going to tell me about your upcoming training?" And my all-time favorite question, "Why aren't you helping me make friends?"

I laugh about it now, but back then I was extremely serious. I was slowly removing God's position as the center of my life and putting Kionicio there. Instead of focusing on God, I kept my focus on Kionicio. I wanted him to make me happy, to make my friends for me, to comfort me, to pray for me, to love me the way Christ loved the church, to honor me, to cherish me. I could go on but for the sake of time, I won't. I was needy because I wasn't happy with myself but was extremely insecure.

The more I expected Kionicio to be considerate and notice my unhappiness, the more he shut down. Our arguments just turned into silence. There was a season that passed when we barely even acknowledged each other. It confused me how one minute we would be crazy in love with each other and the next minute not speak. I felt trapped.

Kionicio worked and seemed to have a life outside of us, and all I had was our family. He had the option to come and go as he wanted. We had one car and he often utilized it. That made me even madder because I didn't have room to be angry and leave. No matter what, I was a mother first. I couldn't just pick up and go, plus I didn't have anywhere to go. We lived on a busy street in Korea. I couldn't even talk to my neighbors because they didn't speak English! I was literally in a foreign land, alone, and unhappy.

I needed an outlet so I talked to my mom a lot! Thank God for Vonage; if we didn't have that phone line, I would still be paying on the phone bill. That's how much I talked to my mom. I stayed up all night on the phone with her sometimes because Kionicio wasn't ever home. I found myself complaining about him, talking ill of our situation, and not taking responsibility for my part. I felt because I read my devotional, attempted to attend Sunday service, cooked, cleaned, and took care of our kids, I was perfect.

I still thank my parents to this day for interceding because without them Kionicio and I would be on different paths.

One of the golden rules of marriage is to always talk to an unbiased party, and thankfully my parents were unbiased. My mom saw a lot of her in me. I was a firecracker! I often turned into the hulk during disputes between Kionicio and I. "Don't make me angry!" I found myself unleashing a side that I didn't even know existed. The godly wife that I wanted to be was often forgotten. I was extremely confrontational, loud, and impatient. I carried fear, doubt, and regret with me throughout my day.

I talked to my mom daily; for the most part, she listened and allowed me to vent. She never judged me or said, "I told you so." She encouraged me back to the word of God and reminded me that no matter what, God allowed Kionicio and I to get married. She said, "During this time you need to stop focusing on what Kionicio isn't doing and instead focus on what you need to be doing for God."

I listened but I didn't want to put her words into action because she had her husband home with her. How could I focus on God if my husband was out and about all times of the night with his friends, and I was home alone with our child and another on the way? I was filled with rage. I often looked at Kionicio and saw red. I wanted him to hurt just as much as I was hurting. I wanted to stop cooking for him, stop paying attention to him, and stop supporting him. Any and everything that came with loving and caring for my husband, I wanted to stop!

After a while my dad got tired of me calling every day and venting to his wife. It got so bad that he would take the phone from my mom and say, "Hey boo! How's it going? You good? All right, well go spend time with your husband, love your husband, and pray over your husband! Remember when you told me and your mom that you wanted to marry him because you loved him? Well, keep God first and handle it. As long as he isn't putting his hands on you, you got the tools to work it out. Love you. Bye!"

The words of my father were a reality check for me. It was like a slap to wake me up. I got off the phone saying to myself, "Uh hellooo, I'm a fixer, so why can't I fix this?"

I took that moment in and concluded that I needed to be real with myself. I needed to sit down and dissect where I was in life, understand what I was feeling, and how I needed to invite God back into the center of my life. I made it a point to sit right in front of the window facing the city, every morning, with giant buildings looking back at me. During the evenings, I often felt like I was looking at Christmas trees because the lights were so bright. Although I was facing a big city, I just saw a canvas of God's creation.

It was a reminder that if God can allow these huge buildings to be built, torn down, and remodeled, then why couldn't He rebuild me? I was away from everyone I knew and face to face with all my mistakes. So why couldn't I allow God to make me over? I wanted Him to tear me down and remodel me like those buildings so that I could be stronger.

I began to read the book of Proverbs, and I journalled every morning and mostly at night. Psalm 1:2-3 reads,

But his delight is in the law of the Lord, And in His law, he meditates day and night. He will be like a tree firmly planted by streams of water, which yields its fruit in its season And its leaf does not wither; And in whatever he does, he prospers.

Just like in God's Word, I needed to meditate on Him day and night so that I could be planted because I had a family now.

The first thing I noticed was that I was burdened by lingering insecurities. All the residue that I carried throughout my life hadn't left. It was just weighing on me, withholding me from the freedom that God had promised me in Him. Jeremiah 2:22 says,

> *"Although you wash yourself with lye, and use much soap, The stain of your iniquity is before Me," declares the Lord God.*

No matter how I tried to fix myself and cover my struggles, God still saw that I needed Him. If I hadn't called on the name of Jesus and asked for forgiveness and direction, I would still be in the same stagnant position that I was in back then. I realized that I had to fall to my face and repent. God began to show me how I messed up in my marriage. I kept rushing Him. I needed to apologize to my parents for removing their covering prematurely as well as shift my focus back to Him.

After crying out to God, repenting, and inviting Him back into His rightful position, I called my parents. I spoke to them both over the speaker phone. I apologized to them and acknowledged that I was wrong for getting married so soon. I wasn't confident in my decision, and it wasn't Spirit-led at the time. I took their guidance and parental covering for granted.

I wanted them to know how much I appreciated and loved them. I was thankful for the relationship I had with my parents; although I was an adult, they hadn't cut me off. I had the opportunity to re-enroll in the school of life, instructed by my parents who were led by the Holy Spirit. My mom encouraged me as a woman of God. Through her words and the Word, I quickly realized that I was going about things all wrong.

I began to feel stronger. I constantly prayed over myself and my home. I kept it clean and anointed my walls and my baby girl. I played Gospel music throughout the day that created an atmosphere for the Holy Spirit to come in and have His way. During this time, I was still pregnant so I prayed over my belly. I wanted my baby to feel the presence of the Holy Spirit. I wanted my daughter who stayed by my side through everything to see how a woman of God should constantly press through no matter what her situation looked like.

During the last stages of my pregnancy, I had a talk with Kionicio. I was instructed by God to address my wrong in our marriage. I didn't have a problem with that because this time I was ready to move on. I didn't want to be sad or feel lonely any more. I wanted to make sure my baby was coming into a peaceful environment. I humbled myself and apologized to Kionicio for my attitude, my impatience, my lack of understanding, and all the pressure I put on him to constantly make me happy. I just wanted to get to a place of love and understanding with him.

Weeks later, the birth of our son arrived, and it was amazing! I had no guilt, no shame, and no overwhelming feeling. I was the mother of a little prince, and I had my princess by my side. Kionicio and I were on good terms, and I felt God really moving in my life. Being a mother was and still is the most amazing feeling ever! There is a difference when we have a child in a mature stage in our lives versus being young and trying to find ourselves. God encourages us to look to Him before we jump into making life-changing decisions. He wants to get all the glory so those situations can be used to encourage someone else.

Months went by and Kionicio was back at work. It was just me and my kids. I seemed to like it that way. I read with them, prayed with them, had my own personal time with God, and sometimes went to church with them. I felt like a single mom in a sense because Kionicio was always gone either for work, basketball tournaments, going out with his friends, or checked out on his Xbox.

Instead of being upset with him, I just tuned him out. It was almost like we were roommates. I began to feel disconnected from him. We weren't arguing as much, but there wasn't any reconciliation. In a sense, I was still lonely. I was working on a better me and my marriage by myself.

I soon experienced the feeling of resentment. I resented Kionicio for wanting to marry me and saying he was going to be everything I wanted. I resented him for insisting that moving clear across the country and the ocean away from my family was a good idea, and most of all I resented the progress he was making in his career. I found myself full of resentment and envy of my own husband. I was bitter and soon forgot every single fruit of the spirit and wise proverb I was studying from the Bible. My plans to make it on my own soon came into effect.

Recap!

I would like to encourage us not to allow others to intimidate us because they have a greater knowledge about certain things than we do. Knowledge comes with experience. And don't feel obligated to fit in. God can really speak to us and work on us during our time of seclusion or loneliness.

Transition can be tough. I was young, seeking a refuge through fellowship at church or my relationship with my husband. Instead of being still and asking God to order my steps in where I should go and what I should do (Psalm 37:23), I was moving ahead of Him. When we are anchored in the Lord, nothing can move us, no one's actions, or bad situations, nothing (Hebrews 6:19). If we find ourselves being sensitive to our surroundings and the actions of others to the point where it keeps us from doing our Father's business, we need to redirect our focus.

My focus was on self, which caused me to act on my emotions. In the process of God cleaning me out, He was finding some issues that I wasn't aware of. As believers, we are battling with our flesh every day so it is apparent we ask the Lord God to:

Search me, O God, and know my heart: try me, and know my thoughts; And see if there be any wicked way in me, and lead me in the way everlasting (Psalm 139:23-24).

God sees things that we aren't aware of. While I was finding my place of peace, I allowed the enemy to interrupt my focus and remind me of everything that wasn't going right.

If we find ourselves having thoughts of someone else and what they are doing wrong, we should immediately go into prayer. Let's ask God to help us direct our focus to Him. We should rebuke the power of distraction in Jesus' name so that we know what God's intentions are in our lives. Remember that He has come so that we might have life more abundantly. We weren't designed to live a life filled with bitterness, chaos, and confusion. He loves us, therefore let's do our best to love those around us.

Seven

Impatiently Lost

I was still stuck in Korea, lonely and planning life after my divorce. Kionicio and I weren't really connecting, and I had yet to make friends. I talked to my friends back home every now and then, but our lives were so different that we really didn't have much to say. They were approaching their graduation dates from college, and I was coming up on my second baby's four-month mark. I was excited for them, but I often thought what life would have been like if I had stayed with my parents and finished school.

It hit me that I was nothing but a stay at home mom. I thought, "When Kionicio and I divorce, I need to have a career!" And it didn't make it any better that my mom was asking when I was going to enroll back in school. One night I was talking to my sister, and she was telling me about her school. A light bulb went off in my head. I decided right then that I was going to enroll back in school and complete my degree!

I enrolled back in school, and I felt a sense of belonging. I attended an online university and was excited about it! Since I didn't talk to my husband much, I directed all my energy into school. I replied to every discussion board, completed every assignment, and made sure my grades reflected my hard work! I started to feel like I was slowly getting myself together. I mean after all, I didn't plan on being married for long, so I needed some stability for me and my kids.

Once again, I missed the point of what God was doing in my life. He was making me over so that I might learn the importance of humility. This was my opportunity to show love and encouragement towards Kionicio, but instead, I often got frustrated and displayed a self-righteous attitude.

As I progressed in school, I noticed that Kionicio wasn't being supportive. If I had a test or an assignment to complete, he wouldn't ask if I needed help with the kids or with making dinner. His routine didn't change. He would come home from work, barely talk to me or interact with our kids, and hop on the Xbox or go play basketball. I was left juggling everything by myself. Me being the prideful person I was, I just took it all on, because I knew that I was going to leave him. I kept my feelings bottled up. Since we didn't argue as much, he felt everything was okay, but little did he know that I didn't want to be married anymore.

As I found refuge in school (not God), I was on the computer a lot. Being on the computer opened the door for social media, and social media allowed me to connect with old friends. I soon reconnected with a buddy from high school—a guy, who was nice and even came to our wedding. I mean he came to our wedding so I didn't think it would be a big deal to casually talk to him. It's not like Kionicio talked to me, so how could a little conversation hurt, right? Wrong! I soon found myself looking to my new friend rather than allowing God to help me with my unhappiness.

Since I told Kionicio every time we talked, I felt justified. When Kionicio went out, I found myself on the computer talking back and forth with my old buddy from high school.

We talked about God and family. He was always respectful and encouraging, which is why I enjoyed talking to him. Eventually my resentment, insecurity, and loneliness began to set in, and I would often ask myself why Kionicio couldn't encourage me the way this guy did. I began to compare my husband to another man.

I was slowly inviting the horrors of temptation to creep into my marriage due to the insecurities I wanted to hold onto. The union between man and woman glorifies the Kingdom. When God created the union of marriage, we gained a divine purpose. It was not only for procreation but also to serve each other. God encourages husband and wife to submit to one another in hopes that we may understand how to stand in love through the weak times. Marriage is unity; it symbolizes a team.

My role as a wife was to be strong, courageous, and kind. When my husband was not at his best, it wasn't for me put myself in the position to be acknowledged by another man but remain in place and love my husband back to his purpose in our marriage. A lot of marriages go through trials and don't last because the strengths, roles, and purpose are not identified. If we don't know where to look for help, we won't get very far in our marriages.

I knew that communicating with my friend from high school was wrong, and it quickly faded. I found myself alone again. I got to a point of throwing the divorce word around when Kionicio and I talked. Since I wasn't happy, I wanted him to verbally know how unhappy I was. He needed to know that I regretted marrying him.

I wanted him to know that I felt he lied to me. He wasn't the man he said he was going to be. I deserved better.

Although I was being honest about my feelings, I was presenting them to the wrong person. Instead of taking time to be quiet and pray, I turned everything into an argument. I was being a quarrelsome wife. Proverbs 27:15 says,

A continual dropping in a very rainy day and a contentious woman are alike.

God gave me multiple opportunities to create an atmosphere of love, encouragement, and holiness for my marriage, but instead I created a rain storm of rage, which always turned my husband away and delayed our union together in Christ. Due to the emotional state I was in, I turned into a contentious woman. To be contentious is when one is confrontational. He/she may look for reasons to provoke or start arguments with others. I took every chance I had to argue with my husband, and it stemmed from unresolved emotions that I brought into our marriage.

It just seemed like I couldn't find a happy point in my marriage. Why did I feel so alone? I thought God was punishing me for getting married so early. Little did I know, God wasn't punishing me—He was giving me multiple opportunities to exercise His Word. If He encouraged me to read Proverbs, which is a book of wisdom, then I needed to apply that wisdom to my life.

Proverbs 3:5-6, Proverbs 21:19, and Proverbs 27:15 (just to name a few) all talk about trusting God and not leaning to your own understanding, as well as not being a nagging and quarrelsome wife. The entire fourth chapter in Proverbs speaks about how important it is to get wisdom at any cost. God was speaking to me the entire time! He wanted me to be wise and knowledgeable about what comes with a marriage

Impatiently Lost

so I could handle it with grace and peace. But once again I was misinterpreting His instructions. I made the Word about me. After I had devotion, I found it odd that Kionicio and I wouldn't talk, or we began to argue. Well duh, the Bible says in James 1:22,

But be doers of the word and not hearers only, deceiving yourselves.

I was deceiving myself! I thought, *Okay I read, I prayed, I'm playing my Jesus music, and look at him (my husband). He isn't doing anything (while shaking my head and turning my nose up at him).* I needed to ask myself why I was so concerned with what Kionicio was doing. I trusted God, didn't I? I believed in His Word, didn't I? Then I needed to put God's Word in action and pray over my marriage rather than nag about it!

I just didn't get it. I used the Bible as a tool for judgment instead of love and understanding. It got to a point where my husband asked me, "How are you reading the Bible and talking about God if you walk around being rude with an attitude?" Surprisingly, for the first time I had no words. The Lord didn't allow me to get upset but to sit in the words of my husband. I realized that Kionicio wasn't the only one who needed to do some adjusting.

While marinating on the words of my husband, I knew that those words didn't come directly from him but the Holy Spirit. When we are missing the direction that is embedded in the Word of God, He will use someone or something to get His point across. He loves us so much and will never give up on us! God allowed the very person who I felt was in need of prayer to remind me that I am no better than him. I was convicted and immediately took some time for myself. I made sure I read and spent time with God every day. I no longer made my relationship with God about Kionicio but about me. I wanted to understand what it was to not only be a woman of God but a wife of virtue.

After weeks went by, I felt lighter. My home was brighter, calmer, and sweeter. My husband and I finally were coming together, spending time together, dating, and going to church together. God was rapidly moving on our behalf. God was always waiting to move in my marriage, but He couldn't move until I stopped leaning on my own understanding. Christ is pure, free, and clear. It is up to us to decide when we are going to "deny ourselves, take up the cross, and follow him" (Matthew 16:24).

The two-year hump of marriage had passed us by, and my plan of divorce obviously didn't work out. I felt like everything was finally getting back on track until Kionicio received orders to go to Fort Carson in Colorado Springs. We were excited but I had to re-adjust myself and prepare for a big change all over again. I was optimistic, hoping that everything I didn't accomplish in Korea would be completed in Colorado. I began to give myself a pep-talk, "Okay, I didn't make friends here, and I wasn't a part of a church home, but everything will be different in Colorado!" Church, friends, and career, here I come!

It was 2012, and I was claiming a fresh start! We landed in Colorado Springs, found our new home a week after being in a hotel, and my husband liked his new unit. Everything was going smoothly. We were adjusting well and even found a church to visit. I still was extremely picky about joining a church and had my checklist ready to go!

Impatiently Lost

The children's ministry wasn't as warm and friendly as I liked, once again the congregation wasn't that friendly, and the new members' ministry forgot about my husband and me for almost six months after we joined! As I have matured in my relationship with God, I know now that those issues are small. If there seems to be an issue or something could be improved, get involved as God directs you and be a help rather than a hindrance. As believers, it is our responsibility to serve one another.

Although the mishaps from my checklist clouded my judgment, my husband loved the church and the pastor. In the past Kionicio didn't go to church with me as much or make his relationship with God a priority. A fire was sparking in him now, and he began to open himself up for growth.

Unfortunately I was so concerned with my own feelings that I wasn't being supportive. We joined and went every Sunday for six months, but after a while, I lost interest in going. I kept thinking there was something better somewhere else. I talked my husband into visiting other churches. In our first year of getting adjusted, we went through a long season of church hopping. It seemed like every church we visited just wasn't right for us. After a while, I gave up. I found myself slowly going back into that dark cave I once prepared for myself in Korea.

There was obviously a pattern taking place. When I got close to a breakthrough, I would get distracted and then find myself trying to fill an unnecessary void that I created! Since I gave up on finding a church home, I also gave up on being a stay at home mom. I was seeking to fulfill something in my life, and I couldn't figure out exactly what it was. I thought I needed a career. Without praying, fasting, or seeking God for wise counsel and direction, I sought a job. This girl was going to be a working woman, a student, a wife, and a mom all at the same time!

Now there isn't anything wrong with being all these great things because women do it every day. But it becomes a problem when we are doing things outside of God's will for our lives. God was preparing me for ministry, and the first ministry I had to learn was in my home with my family. If I couldn't manage my home, then how was I going to do all these other things?

I began to apply to schools for educational assistant positions. Since I was going to school for education, I planned to be a teacher. God had always permitted me to be a strong educated woman who would one day possess a career. I felt it, but once again, here I was rushing His hand in my life.

Although I was premature in my future endeavors, one day after applying for multiple positions, God spoke to me and said not to talk to anyone but to be prepared to answer my phone. I did just what He said, and that same day I received a phone call from the principal of an elementary school and got an interview! What I love about God is that He is always in our midst working things out, but because we as His children can suffer from LPS (Lack of Patience Syndrome), we miss out on a lot of blessings.

About three days later, I went to the interview and got the job on the spot! I was hired to be an Educational Assistant at a school. The women even said they would assist me to become a licensed teacher. The teacher I would be working with was extremely nice and her name was Megan also! I felt that was confirmation.

Impatiently Lost

Now once I accepted the position, the teacher asked me if I would be okay with helping her feed one of her students with a feeding tube. My heart dropped; all I heard was "feeding tube" and "child." My nerves and lack of confidence pretty much paralyzed me mentally and physically. I said, "Oh yes, that isn't a problem." But it was a problem because I was scared! I never worked with anyone who needed extra care in that way, especially a child. I left from my interview feeling discouraged. I questioned my abilities and asked God, "Why did you choose this class for me?" I sounded like a big spoiled brat.

I was due to start a week later but instead of showing up for the Educational Assistant position, I went on another interview for a customer service position—two totally different paths. I allowed fear and doubt to take over and used the amount of money I would be making as an excuse to disregard the blessing God was giving me.

I was a college student who aspired to become a teacher. I would eventually be faced with students from all different backgrounds, who possess a variety of academic and physical strengths and weaknesses. The thing that makes educators so amazing is that they encourage and relate to all students. God had given me that opportunity. Instead of being mature and willing to learn, I ran like a coward into a job that wouldn't serve any purpose in my life and would eventually send me back into a depressive state.

I accepted the customer service job and began to work full time as a phone representative in the retention department. I quickly met two amazing women and started socializing with them on a daily basis. Although I highly disliked the job, God seemed to always put me in positions to serve and glorify Him in everything I did. My newly found sister friends and I began to go to church together, had breakthrough conversations, and developed a bond that was built on our love for the Lord and desire to be better women.

As they began to elevate professionally, I didn't. My sales were low, I began to have chest pains because I dreaded going to work, and I just wasn't good at my job. I realized that this wasn't what I wanted to do or what God had for me. I prayed and asked God to forgive me for being ungrateful when He blessed me with the very job I had asked for. I went against His timing, and He still blessed me when I clearly didn't deserve it. I had to repent, but what was I going to do about my current situation?

Since I was working, we had accumulated more bills—daycare, a second car note, and rent. I couldn't just back out and go back home. After weeks of crying and complaining to my husband, we both made a plan for me to find a new job either in education or childcare. I couldn't help but think back when Kionicio told me not to work and focus on school, but I didn't listen to him. I felt he wanted to control me and I needed to prove to him, along with everyone else, that I was more than a wife and a stay at home mom! Once again, I had to prove this imaginary point, while carrying this huge imaginary chip on my shoulder!

I got out of that job and not even two weeks later, I began working at a Christian daycare. I went from one bad situation into another. The daycare was awful! The staff was mean, and the kids weren't friendly either! Every day I walked into the building and felt the extremely thick tension. I thought since it was a faith-based facility, the people would be nicer. I went home pretty much every night stressed out and feeling down

Impatiently Lost

because I felt out of place. I soon became numb to the foolishness around me and worked hard to pay off bills. I simply focused on getting a pay check.

My parents decided to come help with my kids as my husband and I worked. I was so excited because I knew my kids were in great hands. We even eliminated a major bill—daycare! I went to work while my lovely parents stayed home with my babies. I didn't have to worry about much. Bills were getting paid, my children were taken care of, and I enjoyed the love of my family being together. Since I was surrounded by family and working with babies all day, I began to yearn for a third child. It had always been a desire of my husband and me to have children, so we went for it! I became pregnant and experienced a little peace within myself during this time.

As I progressed in my pregnancy, my husband told me that he had to deploy. We quickly arranged for our children and me to spend time in South Carolina with my parents. I quit my dreadful job at the daycare and ventured off to stay with my parents where I birthed my third child and second prince, Kash Allen Roberson, as well as completed my Bachelor's Degree, graduating summa cum laude! I felt a sense of relief and accomplishment. God was there, guiding me through everything; even when I was making things hard for myself, He was there! Unfortunately, I wasn't in a position to consistently hear His voice.

I received my degree, attended the graduation, and reenrolled right back into school to pursue a Master's degree. Not only did I pursue a Master's degree, but I still wanted to work. I began looking for a job. My beautiful baby boy was eight months, my middle baby was three, and my oldest princess was getting ready for kindergarten. My focus should have been on taking care of my kids and cherishing precious moments that I would never get back. I was too busy filling up a void that couldn't be filled because I was moving in emotions rather than the Holy Spirit.

During this time in my life, I felt lost; I was never satisfied and often took on more than I should have. God constantly gave me paths that led back to Him, but I wouldn't take them. Ignoring His instruction, I applied for another job that once again had nothing to do with my degree. It was another customer service job, and I hated it. I was working with a group of people with whom I didn't relate very well. I became stressed out about that job also and again dreaded waking up and going to work.

Weeks after I began working there, my mom came back down to visit, and she stayed a couple of weeks to help me with my babies. Since I was working full time, I noticed that my youngest baby didn't want much time with me because he quickly latched onto my mom. He was actively crawling, eating table food, and cooing out of this world! I love and adore my children. I always wanted them to know that they are my first priority, and I wanted to be the one to take care of them.

I began to ask myself, *Why are you so worried about contributing financially to the family when the family is not hurting for money right now? Why are you trying to compete and prove something to your husband when you don't have to? Why are missing out on precious moments with your kids when you don't have to?*

During my time of working, we paid off our credit card debt and vehicles. Once again God still blessed my family and me. Since finances were manageable, I didn't have any more excuses. My spirit was extremely weak. I felt like I couldn't think straight. I knew it was time for me to regain my position back in the home and learn to truly appreciate where God had placed me. I had to accept that my life wasn't like everyone else's, that I had a purpose that revolved around God. It was time to surrender and stop making this process so difficult. I had been lost for so long that I didn't really know where to begin.

Recap Time!

During this entire chapter, I was running around like a chicken with its head cut off. I applied to four jobs and worked three different ones within a year. I was so busy trying to be a working woman that I began to lose sight of my actual career goals and most importantly, my family. I was constantly dissatisfied and felt alone while trying to fill a bottomless pit that lingered in my life.

The void that I was constantly trying to fill could only be filled under the direction of God. I needed that connection with my heavenly Father. I needed Him to cover me, but I was too full of myself to understand what He was doing in my life. I made things harder for myself. I brought on unnecessary depression, panic attacks, and arguments with my husband. I even lost time with my children—all because I took control over my own life.

I pray that we are able to enjoy where God has placed us as well as what He is doing in us! I had time with my extended family, birthed a healthy baby boy, completed my degree, paid bills off, witnessed my husband returning from his deployment unharmed, and that still wasn't enough! All these blessings were granted to me even when I didn't appreciate them. God was showing me that He was all that I needed but I ignored Him.

Matthew 16:24-25 says,

> *Then Jesus said to His disciples, "If anyone wishes to come after Me, he must deny himself, and take up his cross and follow Me. For whoever wishes to save his life will lose it; but whoever loses his life for My sake will find it."*

Let's allow Christ to help us regain our lives today! God doesn't want us to feel lost and alone. He wants to bless us beyond what we can ask or think (Ephesians 3:20). He wants to take us out of confusion and uncertainty when it comes to our futures. It may not be clear now, but when we strive to trust God, He will grant us the ability and strength to move mountains! (Mark 11:23)

Eight

Wheeeere's God?

After weeks of complaining, being stressed out, and enduring a season of unhappiness, my husband and I decided that it would be best if I returned to the homefront to take care of our family. I decided to enroll in school full time and focus not only on my family but the completion of my graduate degree online. I felt like I could finally breathe. I didn't want to talk to anyone, go out, or occupy any of my time outside of my home. I found myself staying inside the house all day. I cooked and cleaned every chance I got.

Although I was finally at home doing what I wanted, which was taking care of my family, I still found myself experiencing that lost feeling I often struggled with. The spiritual cave that I once dug myself into became a reality. It became my home. My home was my hiding place. In the past, I would find things to distract me from my relationship with God; this time I allowed my home to fill that void.

I wanted to stay inside so badly that I began to experience anxiety every time the idea of leaving would come about. The furthest I went was to take my daughter to school—anywhere else was my husband's job. Because I was a fixer, I masked my anxiety well. I used cleaning as my reasoning to get out of going everywhere else.

I found it hard to sit still because if I did, I would be

stuck in dark thoughts. I wasn't ready to face the issues I had conjured up in my spirit. I went from cooking, cleaning, taking care of my family, to school, then exercising. These things sound great, but one important thing was missing—my relationship with God. I had managed to move God way down to the bottom of my priority list. My family and I weren't involved in church, and I wasn't reading or praying. I began to truly feel like a hollow shell.

The emptiness that I felt once again began to show in how I treated my husband. The progress we were making in our marriage soon stopped due to the lack of peace I was experiencing within myself. Our relationship with God can be seen in how we treat others. When we aren't practicing the love of Christ, then we won't understand how to love ourselves; and if we can't love ourselves, how can we love someone else? During this time, I wasn't practicing the love of Christ, and in turn, I wasn't loving myself, which affected how I displayed love towards my husband.

I found myself once again lashing out. My moods would change so fast that anything set me off. I was emotionally unstable. I felt like a tornado was running through my mind, and a thunderstorm was flooding my heart. Instead of praying for myself, I often got mad at my husband for not praying for me. I wanted him to see that I was in pain and call out my issues in the name of Jesus! I didn't want to use my own God-given authority because I didn't want to admit that I was the reason why I wasn't happy.

I thought it would be easier if my husband took responsibility for my unsatisfied, entitled attitude. After all, he was supposed to be the head of the house hold, right? Wrong! While I dug myself into a place of hiding, I pushed my husband into a desert of defense. He soon became dry in his communication and defensive every time I spoke to him. We fell back into our old cycle of silence towards one another.

I began to feel drained. It was like a dark cloud of negativity was constantly hanging over my head. When I talked to my parents, they would tell me to get into church, start reading my Bible, and speak positivity over myself. My father told me I needed to prioritize my alone time with God. I heard them, but I didn't want to do what they said. I was so lost in my own way that reading the Word and praying seemed too much for me to handle alone. I felt like I needed help because I didn't even know where to start. I started having demonic dreams of myself not being able to breathe while something was holding me down in a dark room. I was exhausted mentally, spiritually, and physically.

I didn't have friends to talk to, my husband didn't understand me, and I couldn't hear God's voice. I had drowned Him out for so long that I couldn't tell if my thoughts and decisions were God-driven or from myself. I felt blind. Casual thoughts of suicide often popped in and out of my head. I realized that my mental state found a bit of pleasure in being lost in a dark place and wanted to glide to no return. I gave up on myself and lost sight of my purpose.

After months of loneliness and not understanding why I couldn't come out of my sorrow, my husband and I went to go see my doctor. I explained to him what I had been feeling. I was tired of feeling low. I wanted to be happy and fully functional not just for me but for my family. I saw a therapist and was diagnosed with high anxiety and mild depression. I then was treated with Xanax and an anti-depressant. After three weeks, I wasn't as anxious but I wasn't as alive as I knew

I should be. I went from being full of emotions to no emotion at all. I was tired, I barely wanted to talk, and I lost interest in being intimate with my husband. The highlight of my day was going to bed.

After a month of feeling dead, I emotionally broke down again. I cried out to God, asking Him for help and direction. I wanted to hear His voice. I wanted to surrender and strive to serve Him. I yearned to feel His presence. I had been out in the wilderness for too long! I was ready to come back home. I knew right then at that very moment that no amount of medicine was going to cure the darkness that lingered inside of me. The enemy had wanted me dead for a long time, and I was on my way to giving him exactly what he wanted.

I had to accept that God wanted to do extraordinary things with an ordinary person. God had spoken over my life as a child. I had been running from my purpose. I couldn't hear His voice, not because He hid from me, but because I hid from Him. I was covered in so much of my own stink that all the funk muffled my spiritual ears and kept me from my Father's voice.

I had to surrender and ask Him to wash me clean so that I could take responsibility for my life and how I got to this low place. I had so many blessings around me that I couldn't see them. The tiredness and weakness I was feeling was my spirit woman calling out for help. I needed to get my flesh under control and nurture the seed that Christ had planted inside of me. It was time to get out of Megan so God could use me for His glory. He was ready to grow me up. All that time I was waiting on Him when my God was simply waiting on me.

After crying my eyes out and having a true moment of

transparency, I picked myself up and went to work for the Lord. Not only did I have a spiritual cleansing moment, but I cleaned my home with prayer! God told me He was going to prepare me for many teaching moments so meditate on Him day and night. Shortly after receiving those instructions, my mother-in-law came to stay with us for a little while. I had the opportunity to see a spiritual warfare firsthand.

As she was going through her struggles, the Holy Spirit was right there with me, coaching me through every situation, giving me scriptures, telling me how and what to pray for, when to speak and when not to speak. I learned the importance of listening and planting seeds as well as respecting and receiving people where they were.

Once my mother-in-law left, my sister came to stay with us. I then had my second opportunity of a Holy Spirit teaching moment. My sister is a powerful woman of God. During her stay with my family and I, she was battling her own struggles. Her spirit woman would pop in and out. We had a lot of great times while we worshipped in the presence of Christ, but we also had a lot of challenging times. Because I was still learning how to keep myself in line, I made a lot of mistakes when communicating with my sister. God wanted to show me how to apply love to conquer issues rather than get worked up. "Let light shine out of darkness" (2 Cor. 4:6).

When we allow people or situations to get us to a point of no peace, we are no longer wearing our armor of God that prepares us for battle. We are automatically setting ourselves up for failure. And most of all, we throw an opportunity away for others to see Christ in us. Because my sister was going through spiritual warfare, it was up to me to trust God and gradually love her back to Him.

During my time with my sister, I learned the importance of patience. I often tried to fight her battles for her, which turned into me fighting with her. Let's remember that the battle is never ours but the Lord's (2 Chron. 20:15). He died so that we don't have to fight battles. He wants us to simply trust Him enough to apply His Word in every situation, and pray for ourselves and our loved ones, believing that God is going to have the final say (Prov. 16:1).

Just like with my husband, I was getting in God's way when He was dealing with my sister. It wasn't for me to get mad at her or even expect anything from her during that time because I knew she was going through her own little storm. A lot of times we stand in the gap for others when God never asked us to do so, which causes us to get easily burnt out and invested in people's problems that didn't have anything to do with us from the beginning.

Just a little reminder to all of us warriors for the Lord—we are not the only ones God talks to. He talks to all of us every single day in different ways. We shouldn't assume that the one person whom we feel isn't getting it, isn't hearing it (Job 33:14-17). Let God work it out, that's what He does best. It took months after my sister moved out for me to understand how God wanted to use me in her life. I was so caught up in what I wanted for our sisterhood that I pushed the broil button on her cooking time with God. So God kicked me out of the kitchen!

After adjusting to no more houseguests, I found a sense of peace that I hadn't experienced in a while. I was finally content in all areas of my life (Phil. 4:11). I found myself in constant worship, every single day. I was on a routine. My entire life seemed brighter and easier, all because I had cast

Wheeeere's God?

every single care on Him and I felt stable (Psalm 55:22).

Since the homefront was secure, and I felt God moving inside of me, I was ready to break away from my home and go back to church! I still felt a disconnect with a lot of the churches in my location, but God always intervened and guided me exactly where He wanted me to be. I received an invitation to church from an old friend.

During this time, my parents were visiting, and we all were in need of a good confirmation of God's Word. The morning we were preparing for church, I felt a jump in my spirit as if something was going to happen. I couldn't sit still. I was excited! My family and I left to attend a church service that was just down the street from our home. As soon as I walked in, I felt that God had something with which He wanted to remind all of us.

While praise and worship were taking place, the first lady of the church grabbed the mic and began to make her way to the area where my family and I were sitting. She began to prophesy over us one by one. She took her time and allowed God to use her in a mighty way. I immediately felt a connection with her. The gifts that she had dwelling inside of her, I knew that God was mixing something similar inside of me. She was a bold, powerhouse for the Lord and wasn't ashamed to remind you who she was and whom she serves!

I fed off her positive energy extremely fast. She came to me and looked me right in my face and said, "You can't sit any more. It's time for you to get up for God and come out of your hiding place. He has so much work for you to do!" She spoke of the ministry God had been dealing with me about; she even spoke of this very book that I am writing right now. She confirmed everything that God had spoken into my life.

Once service was over, I felt a burning in my belly. I left church, never the same. Under the authority of the Holy Spirit, she stirred up something in me that encouraged me to only move forward. One of the reasons why I love God so much is because He speaks to us in the spirit, but He always sends confirmation through His people. There are people whom God handpicks to guide us back to Him through supernatural abilities. I want to encourage us to look to God, so no matter where we are, we can experience Him in a supernatural way.

Recap Time!

Finally, I got to a place of clarity! Through my struggles with anxiety and depression, I was forced to be still and give God the room He needed to work in my life. He wanted to show me how to depend on Him. I was so used to fixing everything myself that I began to distance myself from God. I wanted to fast forward the moments God wanted me to enjoy. God takes His time with us because He loves us that much! As He is teaching and speaking life into us, He will then begin to confirm His Word through His people!

I claim in Jesus' holy name that we learn to surrender to the power of the Holy Spirit so that we may live out His divine will for our lives! I ask God to send people in our paths at the appointed time who will speak life into our situations and stir up the gifts and talents that Christ has invested inside of us as we began to move forward and never look back. We will have the ability to see God's confirmation through the signs, wonders, gifts, and various miracles of the Holy Spirit according to His will (Heb. 2:4) in Jesus' name, amen!

Nine

Feelin' Myself Again

I was feeling "young and saved"! I received a word from God and a beautiful, prophetess who confirmed exactly what God had been telling me. I was ready to move full force into my calling, leaving behind anyone who would get in my way! (And I did mean anyone.) I was so excited to learn more about what was burning inside of me that I made an executive decision, without the input or concern of my husband, regarding where we were going to serve God.

I found myself moving prematurely once again! I began to get lost in my own self-righteousness, mixing up the roles in my home. My husband already made it clear what church he wanted to attend, and we were members of that church. Instead of having a discussion with my husband, I didn't give him time to think about anything.

I wanted to know what he thought right away, and if he didn't agree with me, I just knew he wasn't giving his all to God (that clearly was an awful assumption). I quickly forgot that I had taken vows and agreed that my husband was the leader of our home.

As his teammate, it was important for me to communicate what I was feeling rather than tell him what we were going to do. It was important that I took his feelings into consideration and show enough respect to speak with him regarding major decisions so we could agree. As husband and wife, we were designed to move as one.

After telling my husband what I was going to do for me and my kids, we ended up attending two different churches. I was going to one while he was at another. We both were learning two different things. Our children often asked why we didn't go to church as a family; and of course, there were assumptions made that my husband was at home while I took my family to church alone. Attending a church without my husband felt completely wrong. God immediately convicted me. Once again God took me through a teaching moment. He showed me what happens when spouses step out of position and aren't aligned together in Him.

No matter how ordained our calling is, our first ministry is in the home. I was divinely called to be a wife and a mother first. God wanted me to understand the importance of order. How was I going to pour into the lives of others if I couldn't even pour into my own spouse? I needed to speak life into my own husband, meet him where he was by attending a church where he was getting fed. I never prayed or consulted with God about where my family was supposed to be. I was out of order by moving ahead and leaving my husband to attend a different church alone.

Although I was receiving conviction pretty much every Sunday, I still attended my church of choice, which caused some friction at home. I often asked my husband to just come to church with me; and he did sometimes. He made it clear, however, that he wasn't going to join because of his growth and obligation to the church we had joined previously as a family. I wanted my husband to give into me and do what I felt was best, but his say was nay.

Feelin' Myself Again

We both began to lead ourselves in the feelings of pride. He was bothered that I went before him and decided to join a church without his involvement, and I was upset that he didn't understand what God was doing inside of me! We didn't pray together. We didn't really eat together. We didn't do anything together. I realized that since our spiritual foundation was separated, our foundation in the home was broken. It all became unbearable, and I had to pray to settle my spirit because I was extremely disturbed and felt an emptiness that I hadn't felt in a while.

After some time of experiencing extreme uneasiness with my husband, God intervened and allowed both of us to talk so that we can find our way back to one another. Even though I knew I was wrong for stepping out before him, my pride was still very present. I still wanted to know that my husband was going to commit his life to God.

I didn't want to leave the church where I felt I could grow spiritually just to feel alone all over again at my husband's church. The resolution to our conversation was for our family to come together and unite under one house of worship. I wasn't looking forward to breaking the news to my new found spiritual mother and pastor, but since I was in the process of being trained, it was important for me to be obedient no matter what it looked or felt like.

Once I separated from my church, I went back to church with my husband. One Sunday, I remember feeling extremely dumb. The pastor was preaching the importance of possessing patience and serving in the kingdom of God. He explained how those of us who possess gifts and talents should be connected to God at all times so that He can take us into a whole new dimension of praise and understanding.

The pastor that day reminded me that we can never be impatient with God and what He wants to do in our lives. If things look grim or don't seem to be moving as fast as they should, we need to just continue to stand on His Word. This was the same church I talked about in the previous chapters, where I didn't feel connected and the children's ministry wasn't consistent. I had an entire checklist of why it was wrong, but not once asked God to direct me on how I could be a blessing to the Kingdom through serving.

When we are looking for a church home, the very first thing we should be focused on is how our spirit receives the Word of God. The pastor who is sharing God's Word should be consistently led by the Holy Spirit, and if that is taking place, everything else will fall in line with the assistance of a faithful congregation. People, such as myself at the time, who come to get fed once or twice a week and then leave are like leeches that just suck everything dry. God didn't design us or His house to be dry but to be alive, warm, loving, and productive! I learned that all in one service. The Holy Spirit was slapping me all upside my head that day but also cradled me in love because God knew I was finally getting to a mature state of understanding.

By this time our stay in Colorado was coming to an end. We recommitted ourselves to church as a family for about two months, and then it was time to pack up and leave to start our new adventure in Hawaii. Of course, now it was time to make my new mover's resolution, "I will join and serve in a church, I will strengthen my relationship with God, I will be on a schedule, and be a better person than I was at the last two duty stations!"

God held me to those declarations. This was our third

move, and I could feel something different approaching my family. I never stopped praying from the time we left our home, to the time we boarded the plane, to the time we landed. Looking back during that time, my prayers were creating an atmosphere for God to move. Not even a month after we were in Hawaii, my husband got promoted, we purchased a second, brand new vehicle, and we walked into our home in half of the time it normally took new residents. God was granting us with an abundance of favor. In the past, I wasn't seeking His face, so I missed out on what God wanted to do in my life but not this time!

Of course, I still had to pray myself out of those feelings of uncertainty, doubt, and fear. The enemy wanted me to slip back into my old habits, but I knew God was bigger and greater! I knew that He was ready for me to walk all the way into His purpose for my life, and I did just that. Once we were settled in our home, we joined a church, and I became active, ready to serve. This time everything seemed to flow. My husband and I were on the same page regarding what we expected from our church as well as from one another. We began to talk more about the Word and how we would incorporate it into the lives of our children. We were finally in our position, having a clear understanding of our roles for the Kingdom inside as well as outside of our home.

Recap Time

There wasn't much drama in this chapter because by this time I understood what God required of me. I got so excited about how God was moving in my life, I got a little beside myself. When God begins to unleash the gifts and talents that He implanted inside of us, changes begin to take place.

We will feel new, different, changed, rearranged, happy, motivated, and on fire for God! I experienced these things but I had to remember the most important thing, humility.

Romans 12:3 reminds us that we shouldn't think more highly of ourselves than we ought to think but to think with good judgment according to faith given by God. This verse is so important to all of us who have accepted our calling and purpose. We all may have a different purpose, accept our positions at different times, but God loves us all the same and our number one purpose should be to edify the body of Christ and not our egos.

Although spiritual gifts were manifesting inside of me, I needed to focus on building up my first ministry, which was my family, and then move into service with my church family (1 Cor. 4:12).

God is so amazing! The moment I realized that I needed to humble myself and receive redirection, He began to move on my behalf! My husband and I began to experience God's favor like never before! James 4:10 says,

Humble yourselves before the Lord and He will lift you up.

He did just that! My God not only lifted me up but my whole family. It's okay when we don't get it right or we misunderstand His direction, but let's humble ourselves so that He can do a new thing in our lives (Isaiah 43:19).

Ten

Full Circle

We were all finally settled in Hawaii—visiting beaches, sightseeing, and eating great food! Most importantly, God led us to a phenomenal church where not only myself but my children began to serve in different ministries. I felt a shift in the atmosphere, and I knew God was brewing up something new for our lives.

I was excited about the new opportunities God was going to present to us while we were stationed in Hawaii, but I still felt out of place, like we were just passing through. In previous discussions I had with my husband regarding his career path, we agreed that he was going to complete his 20 years in the army and then retire. Due to my fear of failure or not rising to our full financial potential, I never entertained the idea of our family transitioning out of the military before the twenty years were up.

For some reason, my mindset began to change. Every time I thought of my family, I could no longer imagine us in the military. In my quiet time with the Lord, I saw and felt us back home in Texas. I felt stability, still ground, rest, peace, and comfort there. When I looked at my husband, I saw him sharing his experiences with other young men, coaching our children's sports teams, and being present for every family event possible. I had to pray and ask God why I was constantly having visions of Texas. God told me then that He was sending us back home as one because we were ready to walk into our divine calling as husband and wife without distractions.

When I heard the instructions of the Lord, I felt a sense of nervousness. I immediately wondered, *Are we going to be able to afford moving back home without the benefits of the military? I am not even working yet!* Before having a conversation with my husband about it, I went into prayer for a couple of days so that I could be focused and clear when this topic came up.

After being released from my time with the Holy Spirit, I told my husband that God was going to release us from the military and send us back home. We both looked at one another with a smirk on our faces and my husband asked, "How do you feel about that?" I expressed that I was a little nervous but looking forward to being stable in our hometown. He then agreed and expressed to me that he never really felt a connection with the military but appreciated the foundation it laid out for our family, our finances, and adding to his growth as a man.

That discussion set the tone for our time in Hawaii. I felt a sense of relief as well as a release of heaviness that had lingered in our marriage for some time. I knew that my husband finally felt that I not only trusted God with our future, but I finally trusted and supported him as the head of our family. We set a three-year plan on how we were going to transition back home fully equipped and ready to move forward into success.

As time went by, God still made Himself extremely present in our home, our thoughts, as well as in our everyday activities. He was constantly directing my decision making. After a year of being in Hawaii, God told me that everything we did would be successful because it would be granted by Him.

I was often nervous because it seemed like His voice became clearer and clearer every time I heard it. And as fear tried to creep up behind me, the words of Deuteronomy 31:6 kept coming to me.

Be strong and courageous. Do not be afraid or terrified because of them, for the Lord your God goes with you; He will never leave you nor forsake you!

God was confirming His presence in my life through His Word. I knew then that it was time to exercise my faith and apply the word of God in everything that I did. He was taking us to a new level, a new dimension of praise, and I was finally ready for what was ahead!

As I moved in the presence of God through His Word, He instructed me to serve in the Youth Department at my church. I had the privilege of teaching the youth alongside a team of young adults who welcomed and encouraged me without any restrictions. God reminded me to stay focused on Him as He revealed what had been sitting inside of me my entire life. I realized that once I sat still long enough, God could begin to use me as He saw fit.

Once I was obedient and acted on His instruction to serve in the youth ministry, He acted on His promise by providing me with a job at a middle school as an educational assistant. Through that job, I had another opportunity to become a permanent substitute for an agency that sent me to a variety of schools throughout the week to work with children who had special needs. I then begin to network with a variety of educators who gave me insight on the education field. I began to see that once I strived towards submission, God began to restore everything that I gave away or passed by due to my lack of patience and trust in Him.

As I grew in my relationship with God, He started to show me that I had to be flexible in Him. I could no longer make situations, opportunities, and most importantly my relationships all about me but instead about Him. Of course, I still had struggles, but I no longer wanted to hide them or fix them myself. I yearned for the correction from my God. I often invited Him into my thoughts and asked Him to direct my decision making. I sought His permission to move throughout my day. I learned how to deny myself on a daily basis. The more I denied myself, the humbler I became. My eyes and ears were open to the spiritual counsel of my heavenly Father.

I wish I could say that since I was more open to God's direction, my time in Hawaii was great. Unfortunately, it wasn't. I found myself coming face to face with more emotional baggage that I didn't even know existed. My entire life I doubted myself and never really had the confidence to boldly move in God's Word out of fear of the opinions of others. We should remember that God wants us to please Him in all we do, meaning that the opinion of man shouldn't matter.

While serving in ministry and working with all kinds of people from different backgrounds, I was challenged to act in the areas in which God had been strengthening me. I found myself no longer being able to run and hide in that cave of seclusion I loved so much but instead use His voice, love, and

Full Circle

patience that dwells inside of me through His Word.

I had a lot of releasing and clarity moments in Hawaii. I saw that God wanted to handle every emotion and insecurity that tried to hold onto me. I didn't only yearn for His peace, but I began to experience it. I valued my alone time with God and stopped caring about the approval of others. I proceeded to be a true servant of God through my love and understanding of who He wanted to be in my life.

Let's remember that if we are only trying to please people, then we aren't true servants of God (Gal. 1:10). God began to make Himself known because I slowly stopped caring about what others thought. I only cared about what my Father thought. When we make God the center of our lives, we should remember His thoughts towards us through His Word. He will keep our eyes and motives set on Him, as we look unto Jesus the Author and Finisher of our faith (Heb. 12:2).

My family and I were rapidly approaching the two-year mark in Hawaii. God reminded me not to get attached but to remain focused. I would often sense that our season was about to change. Learning to break old habits, I had to tell myself to calm down and pray for guidance.

Although I wanted to figure out what God was doing, I couldn't because I gave up my job as the fixer. I stayed to myself and prayed a lot. One night, my husband came home and said he had some news. He told me and our children that we were moving to Arizona in three months! A rush of thoughts went through my head. I didn't understand why we had to leave an entire year early.

After five minutes of silent shock, I reflected on everything God had told me in my time with Him, and it all began to make sense. I was learning how to be flexible in Him, to trust Him, and most importantly not take over His plans for my life. I knew that the curveball that was just thrown us was an opportunity to apply what God had been teaching me. I told my husband that if it was time, then we would trust God and believe that everything would work out.

That night, my husband and I prayed. We both came together for the first time in seven years of marriage, not knowing what or why things were rapidly changing but humbly cast our cares to God. I finally began to understand the importance of possessing supernatural patience because it surpasses our urge to want to move ahead of God. If we are constantly moving ahead of our Creator, we will miss moments to apply His Word and experience the peace and comfort He wants to share with us.

I didn't know what was ahead in Arizona. I wasn't sure where I would work, where we would live, or how my kids were going to like school. I finally realized that it was never for me to have all the answers but to be content in knowing that no matter what, my heavenly Father would take care of everything. As I reflected on my journey from a young girl to a 28-year-old wife and mother, I was excited to finally allow God to take the wheel of my life.

In closing, I want to encourage us all to put down our fears, negative thoughts, past experiences and just try Jesus! Remember what it says in 1 Peter 5:10,

> *After you have suffered a little while, the God of all grace, who has called you to His eternal glory in Christ will himself restore, confirm, strengthen and establish you.*

Full Circle

No matter what we felt we missed out on or gave away, God will restore every blessing and more! It is simply up to us to get out of His way. It still amazes me how He allowed me to walk in everything I ran away from regarding ministry, working in the education field, as well as finding security in my marriage. I will forever embrace the growing pains that I have endured because it shaped my relationship with God for the better.

I'm sure it may seem hard sometimes or we may feel a release only to find ourselves in another bad situation. With the power of Christ, however, He can turn everything around for us, even in the areas of our lives we can't see. He wants us to learn how to fully trust Him. Our commitment to Him, the application of His Word over our lives, and the acceptance of the growing pains that come when we are put to the test of exercising our faith will make us better in every way! I know He is real because He has been carrying me through life since I came out of my mother's womb.

If He can take me out of my dark, dry places, turn my marriage around, keep my children, and continue to give me insight on how to gain the wisdom and knowledge to be prosperous in every way, I know He will do the same for you! A lot of time in our flesh, we think too much about the directions of God. We try to figure things out or have high expectations of ourselves on what we think it takes to be righteous while all God is asking for us to do is come as we are so He can do the rest. He doesn't need our help—just the openness of our hearts.

Remember that God doesn't operate on time. God operates on His love; and if He isn't timing us, then why are we rushing His great works? I speak nothing but life and God's supernatural blessings over our lives and I pray from here on out, we slow down and allow God to work!

God bless you!

About the Author

Megan Roberson believes her purpose is to encourage others to experience the joy of the Lord. She was called to ministry as a teen and continues to serve in the youth department of her church where she shares her experiences to help build a generation on fire for the Kingdom. Megan truly believes that when you are planted in the word of God and seek His direction first, everything else will work itself out.